To Nancy,
With many thanks
for your help!

Merlin

NANCY GIBSON
2712 GLENHURST AVE. SO.
ST. LOUIS PARK, MN 55416

Animalia by Graeme Base © Harry N. Abrams Inc., 1986

Wilfried Schober

The Lives of Bats

ARCO PUBLISHING, INC.
New York

Translated from the German by Sylvia Furness
Revised by A. M. Hutson

© 1984 Edition Leipzig
Published 1984 by Arco Publishing, Inc.
215 Park Avenue South, New York, NY 10003
Library of Congress Catalog Card Number: 83–45641
ISBN 0-668-05993-1

Design: Traudl Schneehagen
Drawings: Michael Lissmann
Manufactured in the German Democratic Republic

Contents

Foreword

Bats—strange beings? They fly with their "hands", they "see" with their ears and hang themselves up to sleep by the toes of their hind feet.

Of all species of mammals living on the earth today, more than 950, that is, approximately one in every five, belong to the order of Chiroptera—"insectivorous" and "fruit" bats. A substantial number! For many years, these animals have been a rewarding subject of scientific research, yielding a wealth of interesting information. Although much fascinating material on the biology of bats has been published in recent decades, the findings, on the whole, have drawn the attention only of a small group of specialists.

Bats alone among mammals have mastered the art of active flight. This has enabled them to conquer a new environment. Hand in hand with the development of the organ of flight, bats have evolved a perfect system of echolocation, by means of which they can perceive obstacles and prey in the darkest night. Because they have acquired the capacity for flight, they are able to undertake migrations of the kind we are familiar with in migratory birds. In autumn, many species of the temperate latitudes leave the summer roosts in which they have given birth to their young, and migrate to frost-free winter quarters sometimes more than a hundred kilometres distant, where they survive the cold season while maintaining their metabolism at a reduced rate.

Most people, even in our highly developed industrial countries, know very little about the way of life briefly touched upon here, or about the diversity of these animals.

Indeed, the very word bat is associated with the idea of mystical creatures that are menacing, that may become entangled in a woman's hair and that bode nothing but ill. Their nocturnal habit and silent flight were undoubtedly responsible for the belief that grew up among many people that bats are in league with the Powers of Evil. For this reason, they have played a major role in the superstitious beliefs of men. Still today, in many countries, bats are quite unjustifiably persecuted and destroyed. Yet only very few species are able to cause any real harm to man and his possessions. The majority of bats are harmless or even positively beneficial.

However, it must be noted with concern that in the last twenty years, bat numbers in the industrial countries of the Old and the New World have shown a steady decline. Fear and superstition are not the prime causes of the reduction in numbers, but to a much greater extent, the increasingly rapid changes in the environment. An animal group that has developed and become specialized over a period of millions of years, cannot adapt itself overnight to new conditions. Everyone should be aware of the danger that exists. Legal measures alone are by no means enough to safeguard bat numbers. Only when people are prepared to take active measures to conserve the creatures and their habitats and to avert dangers that threaten them, is there any chance of preventing these curious mammals from being eliminated from our list of fauna.

The purpose of this book is on the one hand to enlighten and to bring about an understanding of the life of bats, and on the other, to foster a positive attitude to bats among people who are prepared to help in the conservation of these admirable creatures.

Leipzig, 1983   *Wilfried Schober*

Bird or mammal, deity or demon

Two characteristic features of bats, namely their ability to fly and their predominantly nocturnal habit caused them on the one hand to be regarded for centuries not as mammals but as birds, and on the other hand to be looked upon in folkloristic tradition as a symbol of evil and mystery—as indeed they still are to some extent today. Even in the age of the atom and the era of space flight, there are still people who run off shrieking at the sight of a bat, or who ascribe supernatural powers to the creatures.

The old superstition that bats will become inextricably entangled in a woman's hair or will make their way into smoke larders in order to eat the bacon there, has persisted to the present day in many countries in Europe. It is said that among the rural population of Finland, the idea still exists that during sleep, the soul leaves the body and flies about in the form of a bat.

The origin of many prejudices against these harmless animals is difficult to establish. Nevertheless, the blind belief that bats are endowed with magic powers is a deeply rooted one. Ancient man, living close to elemental nature was, after all, enormously impressed by the striking appearance or the physical superiority of animals. Since animals were able to perform feats of which man was incapable, supernatural powers were attributed to them. Among certain tribes living close to nature there still exist today interrelationships between man and animals that are difficult for us to comprehend.

For three thousand years, Christians and Jews have been able to read in Leviticus 11 about clean and unclean meats: ". . . And these are they which ye shall have in abomination among the fowls; they shall not be eaten, they are an abomination: the eagle, and the ossifrage, and the osprey, . . . And the stork, the heron after her kind, and the lapwing, and the bat." In a similar list in Deuteronomy, the bat is again denoted as a bird.

In ancient Babylon, Persia and Arabia, bats were similarly numbered among the birds. A Persian manuscript from the ninth century reads: "Among birds, two were created which have a character different from the others. These are the griffon and the bat, which have teeth within the mouth and which feed their young with milk from the teats." Perhaps the griffon mentioned here is not a mythological creature but a representative of the Old World Fruit bats, the Flying Foxes. An ancient Oriental folk-tale tells how bats were at one time birds which were not satisfied with their outward appearance. Instead, they wanted to be changed into men. Their desire was granted only in part. They grew hair and teeth and developed other human features. But their body continued to resemble that of a bird. The bats were dismayed at this, and ashamed to be seen by the birds. From that time on, in order to avoid meeting them, they ventured out only at night.

There are many stories which tell how bats have attempted by guile to profit from their duality of form—as bird and bat. In the sixth century B.C. the Greek slave Aesop, whose fables brought him fame and freedom, related the following story. A weasel that had caught a bat informed its captive that all birds were its enemies. Quick-wittedly, the victim claimed that it was not a bird but a bat, and so regained its freedom. Some time later, the same bat was captured by another weasel, who this time declared that mice were its favourite food. Once again the bat was able to save its life, this time by maintaining that it was a bird. In another fable, Aesop tells how the birds once waged a war with the beasts of the forest, in which victory went to either side in turn. But at each change of fortune, the cowardly bat aligned itself with the victorious side. When the war was over, neither of the contenders wanted to have anything to do with the bat, and it ended as a solitary creature of the night.

A Roman fable tells the following story: When the birds in council passed an edict to exile bats from the kingdom, the bats claimed that they were mice. Then the birds ordained that all mice were to be held in contempt. Now the bats protested that they were birds. Finally, all the beasts in the land became angry, and the bats feared for their life and thereafter dared to fly out only at night.

Among certain peoples, the bat plays the role of a weather prophet. There are many examples of old peasant lore which links the behaviour of animals and the weather. These dicta undoubtedly have a valid scientific basis. So universal was their acceptance that about a hundred years ago, guidelines for forecasting the weather were still being published by the Intelligence Department of the American War Office which were based on precepts of this kind. Some of those concerning bats were of the following nature: "If bats fly late at night, the weather will be fair", or "When bats flutter excitedly and beetles buzz about, the next day will be a fine one." The curious thing about these "service regulations" was that the officer responsible for the compilation of the rules of this kind dealt with bats under the heading "Birds", although zoologists had long since classified them as mammals.

The fact that bats are not birds but rank among the mammals was expressed by John Swan as early as 1635 in the words:

"(A bat) . . . is no bird but a winged mouse;
for she creeps
with her wings, is without feathers and
flyeth with a kinde of skin, as bees and flies do;
excepting that the Bats wings hath
a farre thicker and stronger skin.
And this creature thus mungrell-like, cannot
look very lovely."

This somewhat unflattering description did little to remove the stigma of evil associations borne by bats.

When man, accustomed to light and sun, finds himself in the darkness of night, and his sense of vision is able to tell him little about his immediate environment, he is inclined to give free rein to his imagination. It is easy to attach an aura of mystery and ghostliness to activities of the night. For instance, the croaking of toads becomes a portent of bad tidings or the cry of the little owl an omen of death. Was it not natural then to associate mysterious powers of darkness with bats which dwell in gloomy caverns, only emerging under the cloak of night to flit silently round trees and dwellings, and to compare their fluttering with the phantasmal dance of evil spirits? It is scarcely surprising that not only owls but also bats were nailed to barn doors to ward off evil, disease and witches.

The devil is sometimes depicted with bats' wings, as is that sinister creature of fable, the dragon. The Roman writer Divus Basilius said: "The nature of the bat is related by blood to that of the devil." Not only evil and mystery but also magic and demonic powers are ascribed to bats. The witch doctors of many primitive tribes wore bat amulets and used parts of the bodies of bats to concoct their mixtures and vile-tasting potions. Their purpose was to ward off evil, to heal diseases or to compel the affection of a loved one. It is said that in Anatolia today there are still those who carry secretly upon their person the bone of a bat as a love charm.

In early Egyptian manuscripts dating from the first century A.D. and in the writings of Arabian scholars and physicians there are prescriptions in which whole bats or parts of the bodies are used. They are recommended as cures for asthma and rheumatism as well as for sore throats and baldness. In India, live flying foxes are sold in the bazaars. The skin of these large animals is removed and placed upon the diseased part of the body.

The gods of the Mayas in Central America were often depicted as figures with the head of a bat. They were usually modelled on Spear-nosed bats (Phyllostomidae). The illustration shows a bat god and a human sacrifice with the heart torn out (from Brentjes, 1971).

This is said to cure lumbago and rheumatism. It seems almost incredible that in the sixties, a news item in the Daily Mail reported that in New York, the authorities had banned the sale of bat's blood in the shops there.

Since nothing was known about the bat's capacity for ultrasonic navigation until a few decades ago, it was generally believed that all species of bats had nocturnal vision. Some well-meaning recommendations were, of course, derived from this. For example, in the thirteenth century, in his book *De mirabilibus mundi* (Of the marvels of the world), Albertus Magnus wrote:

If thou wilt see a thing drowned,
or se depe in the water in the
nyghte, and that it shall not bee
more hyd to the than in the daye
and readde bookes in a darcke night.
Anoynte thy face with the
bloude of the Reremouse or backe
and it shal be done that I saye.

(From the *Boke of the mervels of the worlde* translated from Latin and published in London, 1560.)

In the Middle Ages, these "witches' birds" often brought ruin to the people in whose houses they lodged. In the popular imagination, witches and bats had become so closely linked that many an unfortunate soul in whose home bats had found shelter was accused of being a witch and even punished by death at the stake.

In the ancient civilizations of Central America, bats played an important part in the history of religion. One of the deities of the Mayas was Zotzilaha Chamalcan. This god was represented in the form of a man with extended bat wings and the head of a bat. He is depicted on altars, stone columns and on a large number of earthenware vessels which have been excavated in the vicinity of the temples that were built some two thousand years ago. In the picture writing of the Mayas, the hieroglyph for "bat" occurs frequently. It consists of very clearly recognizable bats' heads, the bats usually featured being representatives of the Spear-nosed bats and Vampires. For the faithful who looked upon blood as food of the gods to be obtained by human sacrifice, the blood-sucking Vampire bat must have appeared as a god. Yet the bat chosen to serve as model in the original graphic representations and to be revered as a "blood sucker" was the Spear-nosed bat, probably because its facial appearance was so much more bizarre. To the ancient Zapotecs, the bat was the god of death. For this reason, many burial urns and grave reliefs bear the form of bats. The Underworld Kingdom of Darkness and Death was ruled by the Death Bat Cama Zotz, and all who ventured to descend into this kingdom were slain by him.

Although these gods and their legends have lost their significance in the Central America of today, the old Mayan word for bat has not yet been forgotten. In the uplands of Guatemala, there is still a tribe with the name of "Zotzil" (belonging to the bat). Their god is the bat and their capital city Zimacantlan (the Place of the Bats).

The bat as a heraldic animal. Coat of arms of the town of Valencia in Spain. It is the emblem of the royal house of James I of Aragon (thirteenth century).

Among various peoples still very close to nature, the bat serves as a totem figure. It is believed to possess supernatural powers and is revered accordingly. In the same way, the bat holds a special place in the culture of the North American Indians. One of their traditional stories tells how a powerful and proud warrior, who had been cast ashore on a craggy coast, was saved by a bat in the guise of an old man or old woman.

The Californian Indians believed that they could locate the source of a fire with the help of bats. They also claimed that a bat which has eaten volcanic rock can spew forth particularly fine arrows. From this, one can con-clude, as the American bat specialist Allen writes, that the Red Indians were very familiar with the Californian Long-eared bat which bears on its nose a quite distinct, arrow-shaped cutaneous outgrowth.

Not only did bats make their way into the religious and intellectual history of various peoples, but also into the works of certain leading writers. In his epic poem describing the wanderings of Ulysses, Homer himself made use of the simile of the bat. On his travels which were to lead him home from the Trojan Wars, Ulysses descended into the Underworld. So greatly did he disturb the "shades" that they flew after him fluttering like bats startled from a tree.

Many of the writers of antiquity in whose works bats appear also link them with the forces of evil. Characters who deserve punishment may well be turned into bats. Portrayals of this kind kept alive the antipathy to these animals felt in wide circles of the population.

Shakespeare mentions bats quite frequently in his works. In *A Midsummer Night's Dream*, Queen Titania lets her fairy attendants fashion cloaks from the "leathern wings" of bats. The three witches in *Macbeth* brew a poisonous draught of ingredients which include

"Eye of newt, and toe of frog
Wool of bat, and tongue of dog."

In children's rhymes found in the Anglo-American linguistic area, the bat is often mentioned, frequently with an allusion to its fondness for bacon. This notion has even provided the vernacular name of "bacon mouse", although it appears to be quite unsubstantiated.

Feelings of aversion to bats are all too frequently exploited in film and television. In horror films, bat-like creatures fly across the screen and their ghastly appearance and gigantic size increase the loathing felt for these animals. The bats torture their victims in gloomy cellars or serve as accomplice and tool of the powers of darkness. We need only recall the figure of Count Dracula who, with his vampires, has struck terror into the hearts of thousands.

Yet there are exceptions to this general rejection. In their wisdom, the ancient Chinese placed the bat in a position of high esteem. In China it became a symbol of happiness, and the word "fu" (bat) is also the term for happiness. In their paintings and carvings, Chinese artists made wide use of the bat as a decorative element. Bat medallions are found embroidered on Oriental robes. A talisman commonly worn in China is in the shape of a coin bearing the symbol of the Tree of Life (a tree with roots and branches) around which five bats with wings outspread are arranged in a circle. This talisman of the five bats, called in Chinese a "wu fu", symbolizes the greatest joys of man, contentment, happiness, prosperity, health and longevity.

Bats are also revered on Bali, where the flying foxes that live in thousands in the temple grottoes are protected from all disturbance.

Animal worship and animal cults played a particularly important role in Ancient Egypt. Animals considered sacred included the bull, dog, jackal, snake, ibis, scarab and many others. But remarkably enough, neither the Pharaohs and priests nor the peasantry represented bats as godlike beings. Yet the creatures were not at all rare,

The Chinese look upon bats as bearers of good fortune. Detail from an eighteenth-century robe shows ornamentation in which five bats encircle a Tree of Life. They incorporate the concepts of Health, Prosperity, Long Life, Happiness and Contentment.

for they inhabited the temples and burial chambers in their thousands. Realistic portrayals of bats in wall paintings some 4000 years old also show that the creatures were by no means unfamiliar to the Egyptians.

The examples given here of the centuries old interrelationship between man and bat belong mainly to the sphere of fable or religion, yet for us today they can prove just as interesting as the most impressive results of recent scientific research on bats.

Are bats flying mice?

It has taken a long time for bats to find their place within the animal kingdom scientifically confirmed. In the sixteenth century, the naturalist Konrad Gesner of Zurich wrote in his *Historia Animalium*: "The bat is an intermediate animal between a bird and a mouse, so that it can reasonably be called a flying mouse, although it can be numbered neither among birds nor among mice, since it has something of the form of both." Today this statement seems a curious one, although there are still people who are not too sure what kind of animals bats really are. Indeed, superficial examination reveals characteristics of great similarity between bats and mice. In the case of our indigenous species, we need think only of the size of body, the colour of the fur, the shape of the ears. Over and again we are struck by this similarity to mice and it is sometimes reflected in the names given to bats, as for example, the Large Mouse-eared bat *(Myotis myotis)*. Indeed a whole genus of bats bears the Greek name *Myotis* which simply means "mouse ear". In other countries as well, the popular names for the Chiroptera show that these animals were likened to mice or indeed regarded as such. In Germany a bat is a *Fledermaus* (flutter mouse), in France a *chauve-souris* (naked mouse), in Mexico bats are called *ratones voladores* or flying rats, and old vernacular English names include flittermouse and reremouse.

The scientific name for this order of mammals is Chiroptera, in English, "hand wings". This refers to the most important feature common to all species that are included in the order: the development of the front limbs into an organ of flight. In the process, the forearm, the metacarpal bones and the second to fifth fingers have been greatly extended.

The English zoologist Edward Wotton, a contemporary of Gesner, was the first to recognize the true nature of bats and to classify them as mammals. However, the exact position of the bat within this class, represented a considerable problem to zoologists.

Some 250 years ago, the Swedish physician and naturalist Carl von Linné (Linnaeus) began to make the first comprehensive systematic survey of minerals, plants and animals. Starting out from the concept of "species" which in each case comprises all those animals which are mutually fertile, he classified living beings into a system based on degrees of relationship. His great work *Systema naturae* was first published in 1735. At that time, Linnaeus recognized six species of bat; two each in Europe, Asia and America. At first he classified them with the carnivores, basing his grouping upon characteristics of dentition—many species possess extremely sharp teeth. Later, Linnaeus met with a seventh species, the Fisherman bat from South America, which he placed among the rodents. Since new criteria were constantly being established that were of significance for the classification of animals, Linnaeus' book underwent frequent revision. It is not surprising that at a later stage he replaced the class Quadrupeda (quadrupeds) by that of Mammalia (mammals), recognizing that whales also belonged to this group. Thirty years after bats had first been described, he placed them among the primates, which were further subdivided into four categories: Homo (man), Simia (ape), Lemur (lemuroid) and Vespertilio (bat). Linnaeus based this classification upon the location of the lacteal glands.

The material available to Linnaeus at that time was much too meagre for him to recognize that these animals constitute an order of their own among mammals. But it was only a question of time before the correct zoological classification of bats could be achieved.

After Linnaeus there followed an epoch of discovery and description of new species of animals, in which fresh impetus was given to faunistic and systematic research.

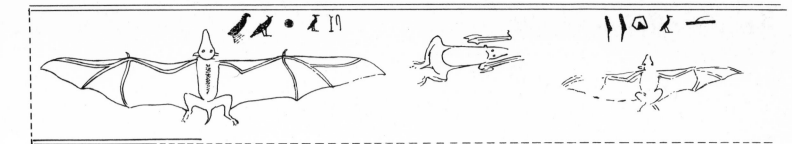

Wall painting with bats (Emballonuridae). These paintings were found in a tomb near Beni Hasan (Egypt) and date from 1800 B.C. (from Brentjes).

Thus began the age of voyages of discovery and expeditions to foreign lands. One result was that over the next 100 years, valuable zoological material, including of course that concerning bats, was gathered, evaluated scientifically and, as a consequence, knowledge of species was enormously enriched.

When the zoologist Koch published his book *Das Wesentliche der Chiropteren* (A Fundamental Study of the Chiroptera) in 1863, he already knew of more than 300 species. Of the Megachiroptera, the Old World Fruit bats, some 50 species were known at this time.

The discovery and description of new species has continued throughout the last hundred years. In all the great museums of the world, specialists are working on bats and reporting on new species from areas of the world that until now have been virtually inaccessible. Specialized literature shows that at the present time there are some 950 species of bat in the world.

The evolution of this group of mammals over millions of years has produced a vast diversity of form. In respect of number of species, bats are surpassed only by rodents —"mice" in popular terms—with some 1800 species.

The development of such a wealth of species within the order of bats can be attributed primarily to the acquisition of the ability to fly. The same phenomenon can be observed in the other members of the animal kingdom that are capable of flight, namely birds and insects. These classes also have an enormous number of species, and have established themselves in the most varied of biotopes. But whereas most people are aware of the great diversity within the bird and insect world, only few know anything about the variety that exists among bats.

Another factor that has furthered this development is that because of their mode of locomotion, it was not necessary for bats to compete for food with the great army of rodents. No bat eats grass or leaves. And competition with birds could not arise since the latter are active for the most part during the day, whereas at night, air space belongs almost exclusively to the bats.

The numerous species that make up the order Chiroptera are classified by the systematist into 16 to 18 families. It is not possible to specify an exact number here since those features which suffice in the opinion of one taxonomist to justify the establishment of a new family may not seem adequate to another. On one point though they are all in agreement, namely that Chiroptera fall naturally into two suborders. The first is the Megachiroptera, the generally large forms known as fruit bats or "flying foxes" (Eisentraut's *Flughunde*, flying dogs). In these cases, the names again show a comparison drawn with an animal that was already familiar. And indeed it is possible to see similarities between the head or face of many of the Megachiroptera and that of a fox or dog. The Flying Foxes inhabit the tropics and subtropics of the Old World; the number of species living today is given as 175.

The second suborder is that of the Microchiroptera, the mainly small forms (Eisentraut's *Fledermäuse*), those known simply as bats or sometimes insectivorous bats. Their feeding habits are varied, their distribution world-wide.

Bats evolved with the dinosaurs

1 *The Temptation of Saint Anthony in the Grotto* by David Teniers the Younger (1610–1690)

The capacity for flight has been developed by bats as a secondary acquisition. Their ancestors were almost certainly quadrupedal mammals. So the interesting question arises "When did these ancestors live, and what did they look like?"

It is necessary to go far back in the history of the earth and in the history of mammalian evolution to find an answer. If man had lived 50 million years ago, he would —as fossil finds prove—even then have seen bats which looked virtually indistinguishable from the species we see today. Bats, then, are a very ancient though highly specialized group of mammals.

In order to reconstruct the evolution of these experts in flight, it is interesting to ask whether there are some other species among mammals living today which have also attempted to conquer the air and could be considered as possible predecessors. And we can indeed find representatives in various orders which show signs of incipient development of flight membranes. Among marsupials, whose best-known representatives are the kangaroos, there is the group of gliding possums or phalangers. They vary greatly in size, but all of them possess a broad fold of skin stretching between the fore and hind legs, forming a patagium, which, when the legs are spread, acts as a parachute, carrying the creature on a gliding flight down through the air. It is not inconceivable that this passive, parachuting flight could represent a preliminary stage in the development of active flight, but the marsupials are such an ancient and isolated branch in the mammalian genealogical tree that there can be no question of their having been ancestors of the bat.

What about the "gliders" among the rodents? In both the Old World and the New, the rodents have produced several species that can be grouped under the name of "flying squirrels". Compared with the phalangers, their adaptation to flight shows some further advances. First-ly, the flight membranes at the sides of the body are broader, and secondly, additional skin flaps have developed between forelegs and neck as well as between hind legs and tail. Anatomical refinements in the structure of this "flight organ" show that it is not invariable in form in all flying squirrels. But the most important point —and this is true also of the phalangers—is that the fore limbs show none of the alterations in the region of the metacarpal bones and fingers that are typical of the Chiroptera. Since adaptation to gliding flight is a secondary acquisition in flying squirrels, and in any case, there is no possibility of rodents being the ancestors of bats, they too can be ruled out of our considerations.

Among mammals, a third group remains which shows clearly the development of a flight membrane or patagium. These are the "flying lemurs", colugos or cobegos of Southeast Asia. The two species so far described are such oddities among mammals that systematists place them in an order of their own. They are, however, more closely related to bats than are marsupials or rodents.

The patagium extends from the neck along the fore and hind limbs and then to the tip of the tail. But these species are not capable of powered flight. Still more significant is the fact that even the colugos show no sign of extension of the finger joints. The patagium does not extend between the fingers. It is precisely this characteristic which, in the case of bats, is a typical feature of the development of the fore limbs into real wings.

Of all the "gliders" living today, none fits in with the line of evolution which has been followed by our bats on their path to active flight. The bonds existing between bats and other mammalian orders in which "gliders" have evolved, are very tenuous. Examination of their "flight organs" is merely in the nature of setting up a prototype to provide suggestions as to how the flight organ of bats might have developed. In all, it can be said

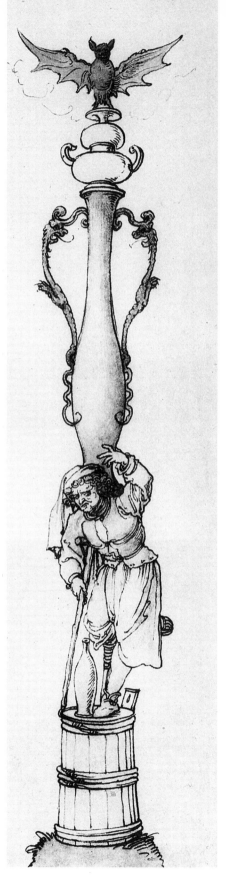

2 A devil with the wings of a bat presents a child as a sacrificial offering to an elephant-headed demon. (French illustration to *The Arabian Nights*. Stuttgart, 1838)

3 *Saturnian Column*. Among the drawings of Dürer are some in which bats are depicted to suggest magic and mystical associations.

18

Following page :

6 Wall hanging with representation of a bat god.
Folk art of the Cuna Indians of the San Blas Islands (Panama).
Murcielago is the Spanish word for bat.

7 Raffia basket with bat motif. Woven by Maidu Indians on the north-west coast of the U.S.A. (about 1880)

8 Representations of fabulous animals also show hybrid beings with the wings of bats.

4 *The Siren of Ravenna*.
A hybrid being with the wings of a bat

5 In the visual arts, Evil is frequently depicted in the form of witches and devils with the wings of bats. This drawing is Number 48 of *Los Caprichos* by Goya, entitled "The Blowers".

that among the species of mammals living today, none can be considered as the probable ancestor of the bat. In order to obtain information about the evolution of bats and about their forebears, it is necessary to consider results obtained from palaeontological research.

What is the situation as far as bats are concerned? Among the numerous mammalian fossil finds, there are some fossils of both major divisions of bats. But in comparison with the fossils of some other groups of mammals, they are not very numerous. The reason for this paucity of fossil evidence could well be that many Chiroptera were inhabitants of tropical forests where, after death, they would be devoured in their entirety by the vast army of ground-dwelling organisms. A more favourable environment for fossilization is provided by caves, although here again, finds dating back several million years are rare. Some of the fossil remains of bats excavated up to now have been in a very good state of preservation. The earliest date from the middle Eocene epoch; that is, they are about 50 million years old.

Because of the excellent condition of some of these fossils, it has been possible to establish that the creatures living at that time had very much the appearance of the species of today. Body form and proportions were basically identical. Forearm, metacarpal bones and fingers are lengthened, and dentition resembles that of the insectivorous bats living today.

A skeleton, completely preserved, of the earliest known bat (Icaronycteris) dates from the early Eocene in Wyoming, U.S.A. It combines features of the two present-day suborders of bats. Accordingly, it is clear that as a type, the bat went through a single process of evolution and this process was already completed some 50 million years ago. The great antiquity of the order of bats is underlined by the fact that it was another 42 million years before the first ape-men evolved on the earth.

Fossil bats from the Eocene have also been found in Europe. In most cases, strata that have been found to hold a wealth of fossil material are those containing gypsum, lignite or mineral oil, laid down millions of years ago in lagoons or great inland lakes.

One of the famous sites of fossil finds of vertebrates in the Federal Republic of Germany is the former oil-shale mine at Messel near Darmstadt. More than a hundred years ago, miners excavating here discovered the first remains of fossil fauna from a tropical-subtropical primeval forest. Careful excavations recently carried out show that all the animals are in an astonishingly good state of preservation, probably because the deeper layers of water in a lake contained no oxygen, as a result of which decomposition of any animal which lay on the bottom was impeded. In addition to fish, reptiles and birds, complete skeletons of insectivores, rodents and primitive horses were found in Messel. It is the fossil bats in which we are particularly interested. The exceptional state of preservation of the skeletons, indeed even of remnants of soft parts with wing membrane and fur, confirm that the general structure of these creatures corresponded closely to that of present-day genera. In some of the bats found, it was even possible to analyze the contents of the stomach. The presence of tegulae (wing scales) is evidence that bats fed on moths even at this time. From this, it can be concluded that the creatures had already evolved an efficient system of echolocation.

A rich source of vertebrate finds from the Eocene was the lignite deposits in the Geiseltal region near Halle (German Democratic Republic). Since humic acids of plant origin liberated in the process of carbonization will normally dissolve bone, so that no remnants are preserved, conditions must have existed here which made it possible for the dead organisms to undergo rapid preservation. In the Geiseltal region, it is very probable that the calcareous ground waters which penetrated from the surroundings into the bog, counteracted the destructive action of the humic acids. A further factor was that the animals died quickly in floods and were embedded in mud; since bacteria and oxygen were excluded, decomposition could not take place. As a result, fragments of skin, feathers and hair can still be distinguished in addition to the bones. The thousands of exhibits in the Geiseltal Museum in Halle provide a glimpse of a tropical fauna and flora inconceivable today, which existed in this region some 40 to 50 million years ago. In addition to plants and invertebrates, the Geiseltal also held fish, amphibians, reptiles, birds and numerous mammals concealed within it. There are fragments of 25 specimens of bats, most of which were excavated during the thirties. Some are complete skeletons, others skull and bone fragments. The entire material is assignable to the species *Cecilionycteris prisca*. Geiseltal bats show certain primitive characteristics of dentition, although the development of the flight apparatus scarcely differs from that of modern bats.

The earliest known fruit bat *(Archaeopteropus)* was found in Italy and is assigned to the Oligocene; that is, it is about 40 million years old. But the separation of the fruit bats from the archetypal bats happened earlier than this. Various characteristics such as the longer skull and the invariable retention of a claw on the second digit have given rise to the conjecture that the Megachiroptera may be more primitive than the Microchiroptera. This assumption has, however, recently been questioned on the basis of extensive examinations carried out on the brains of fruit bats and insectivorous bats. The brain of the fruit bat is undoubtedly more highly developed. In addition, the fruit bats exhibit so many features of specialization (reduced dentition, large eyes, regression of the tail and tail membrane), that they cannot possibly provide a model for the primitive form of the bats of today.

Even though bats evolved to become a distinct group more than 50 million years ago, developments have continued to take place since then. There has been constant refinement of apparently primitive features, adaptation to new biotopes, specialization in respect of feeding, and—of vital significance for the bats—extension of their ultrasonic system of orientation.

Within the system of mammals, the order of insectivores includes the most primitive of mammals which possess a placenta. The ancestors of today's hedgehogs and shrews can also be considered as the forebears of all other placental mammals that inhabit the earth today. It is not easy to imagine that the ancestors of, for instance, great beasts of prey or elephants, of whales or ungulates might well have been shrew-like animals. Yet a wealth of fossil finds dating from various geological epochs has led palaeozoologists to this conclusion. Bats hold a position very close to insectivores. Apart from the capacity for flight and adaptations to particular ways of life that were acquired later, many species still exhibit primitive characteristics. These include skull structure, dentition, the degree of brain development and the uncomplicated structure of the intestinal tract. Therefore it is beyond doubt that bats are derived from a primitive insectivore-like stock. Existing fossil finds show that such forms lived as long ago as in the Upper Cretaceous period, that is, at the threshold of the Caenozoic era some 70 million years ago. Since the earliest finds of fully developed bats date back 50 million years, the process of branching off from the original insectivores must have taken place before this. The ground was prepared in the Upper Cretaceous for the development which was to make the Caenozoic era into the Age of Mammals. In addition to insectivores, new arrivals on the scene included lemurs and the ancestors of the ungulates. They were mostly creatures of small stature, leading a secretive existence, for

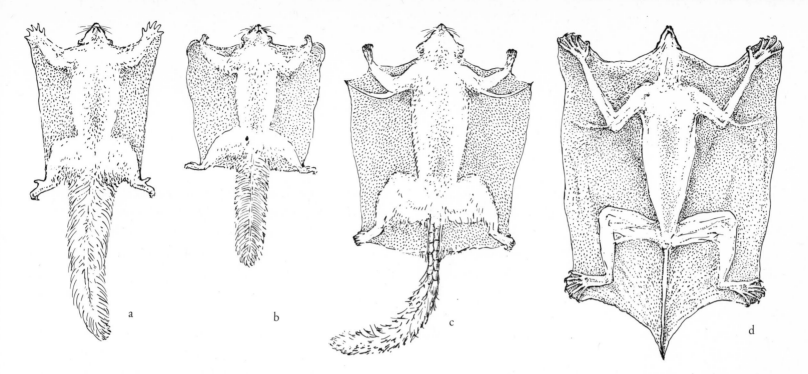

Various kinds of gliding mammals
a flying phalanger or gliding possum *(Petaurus breviceps)*;
b flying squirrel *(Glaucomys volans)*, the flight membrane is extended by a gristly rod at the wrist;
c African flying squirrel *(Anomalurus* sp.), the patagium is given tension by a rod of cartilage extending outwards from the elbow which acts as a strut;
d colugo or cobego, misnamed "flying lemur" *(Cynocephalus* sp.)

they still lived under the shadow of the mighty dinosaurs. Not until these great saurians became extinct, was the way clear for an explosive advance in the development of mammals, which, as we can see today, led to an enormously vast abundance of forms.

In members of various orders of mammals, there are indications of incipient evolutionary development of flight capacity, but only bats achieved true flight. At what stage this occurred, we do not know. From what is already known about the genealogical history and embryological development of mammals, it is possible to gain some simplified picture of the kind of varied adaptations that might have produced flying mammals. Primitive arboreal insectivores undoubtedly were the starting point. The claws on their feet made it possible for them to climb easily and safely up tree trunks and along branches with the sort of skill shown by the squirrels of

today. Their life was spent almost entirely in trees and they became experts in leaping from branch to branch. Since they fed on insects, they would doubtlessly have attempted to catch flying species as they leaped. The gliding mammals mentioned above are also tree dwellers. Although there can be no question of a phylogenetic link with the bat, these examples may perhaps provide some clue to the kind of biological developments that could have led to the evolution of active flight. It is conceivable that the extensive parachute-like flight membranes which make gliding flight possible predated the evolution of the flight organ in bats. A glance at the embryogeny of bats supports this assumption. It is an old biological precept that embryonic development (ontogenesis) passes through the same stages in much abbreviated form as evolutionary development (phylogenesis). What can we learn in this respect from the embryology of bats? In the early stages of growth within the womb there is an initial development of folds of skin along the sides of the body, and only after this do the bones of the fingers begin to lengthen. The wing of the new-born bat is still undeveloped. It is only after a period of growth outside the mother's body that the hand of the young bat reaches its final proportions.

During the course of evolution, when those elements that proved an advantage in coping with the challenges of

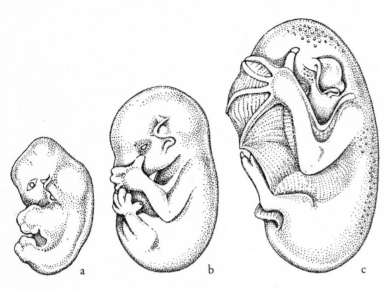

Embryos of Large Mouse-eared bats *(Myotis myotis)* of different ages.
Crown of head to rump length: a 9 mm, b 12 mm, c 17 mm.
Stage c shows the beginning of the modification of the fore extremities into
an organ of flight. The first elastic membranes between the bones of the arm
and fingers are developing (after Schumacher, from Grassé, 1955).

life prevailed and were transmitted, a process began in which the metacarpal bones and fingers lengthened. Undoubtedly this evolutionary feature proved useful. When the fore legs were straddled out stiffly, the wing membrane which stretched between the fingers and extended along the back legs to the tail, functioned as a lifting surface. The flight membrane proved advantageous to the creature when it was catching insects in gliding flight, since it increased manoeuvrability and enhanced the bat's efficiency as a hunter. Once the lifting surface had reached a certain size, the next stage followed in which it could be raised and lowered by the specially adapted front legs. Active flight had become possible. The bats, as a new kind of mammal, had taken possession of the earth, and, like birds, could lift themselves up into the sky.

Flight

Among vertebrates, bats as well as birds have been able to conquer the skies in active flight as a result of modification of arm and hand into a flight organ. But comparison of the bat's wing with the flight organ of a bird or with that of the extinct pterosaurs, shows greater similarities in structure to the pterosaurs. Birds have achieved the capacity for flight by different modifications in the structure of their fore limbs.

In bats, tension and support of the wing membrane is achieved primarily by the arm and hand. In the pterosaurs, only one finger (the fourth) is involved in the system of support and tension, whereas in bats, both the extended fore arm and the entire vastly elongated hand play a vital part. The thumb is something of an exception, for it has not been lengthened along with the other digits. In the Microchiroptera, it is the only finger still to have a claw; the Megachiroptera still have a claw of this kind on the end of the second finger.

In contrast to those of birds, the fore limbs of bats have not lost their significance for locomotion on the ground, in spite of their modification into organs of flight. The powerful claw of the thumb enables bats to climb with great agility along roof timbers or among rocks in caves, and the fruit-eating species to seize fruit and carry it to their mouth. But not only are bats skilful climbers, they are also able to walk on the ground, supporting themselves on the joints of the wrists. It is curious to see how they draw their folded wings along the ground beside them. This locomotion on all fours shows little of the skill usual among mammals.

In spite of being winged, bats are also able to swim to a certain extent. So it is not too serious for them if they accidently land in water. In addition to their function in walking and climbing, the hind legs play another important role. With their sharply pointed, curved claws they serve the bats as hooks by which the body is suspended.

In America and Madagascar, there are certain species which possess sucker-like discs on the thumbs and back feet, by means of which they are able to maintain a hold on smooth surfaces. The bats' ability to suspend themselves in a head-down roosting position, often with the belly against the support, is possible only because the legs of bats, unlike those of other mammals, are directed backwards from the hips.

If a man tried to hang by the toes on wall bars in such a way that his belly lay against the wall, he would not be able to do so. It would be possible only if the knee or foot joints could be turned outwards. In bats, this is precisely what has happened to the hind limbs. Since the leg can be flexed at the knee joint both upwards and outwards, it can take up a position which makes such suspension possible. This rotation of the hind limbs is also an advantage in flight, since they can participate in the movement of the wings.

But to return to the fore legs. The X-ray photograph in Ill. 13 clearly shows the modification of the skeleton of the hand into an organ of flight, and the drawing on page 28 illustrates the essential functional modifications in the anatomy of the fore limbs of bats.

The wing membrane, the patagium, which extends from the side of the body both between the fingers and between the limbs as far as the tail, can be divided into different parts. That part which extends in front of the wings proper along the front edge of the upper and lower arm, is the forward or antebrachial membrane (propatagium). Between the arm and hind margin of the wing is the arm membrane (plagiopatagium). The part which extends between digits 2 and 5 is called the finger membrane (dactylopatagium or chiropatagium). The tail membrane (uropatagium) stretches between the hind legs and the tail. The latter is often supported by a spur extending from the foot joint, the calcar. In certain species of bats, the uropatagium is reduced, and in some groups the tail projects freely as in a mouse. This particularly striking feature has earned them vernacular names such as Free-tailed bats or Mouse-tailed bats. In fruit bats, the tail vertebrae are absent and the tail membrane is only rudimentary.

Embryonic development shows that the wing membrane develops from a fold of skin on the body. Although this double membrane is very delicate, being no more than 0.03 mm thick in small species, it encloses a large number of blood vessels, nerves and elastic fibres as well as small muscle bundles. The muscles of the wing membrane do not contribute to locomotion, but have a supplementary bracing effect and prevent wing flutter caused by air flow. They also facilitate folding of the wing membrane when the bat is at rest. Usually this is achieved by drawing the wing membranes close to the body, while some species wrap themselves in their wings as in a sleeping bag. Since the extensive surfaces of the patagium play an important part in heat regulation, a great variety of different wing positions can be observed among roosting bats, particularly fruit bats, depending upon the external temperature.

In comparison with the feathered wings of birds, the fragile hairless patagia seem much more susceptible to injury. Yet the elastic fibres lend them enormous strength. In addition, the regenerative capacity of an injured patagium is very high. Holes 2 cm in diameter in the wing membranes of captive fruit bats have knitted together again within 28 days.

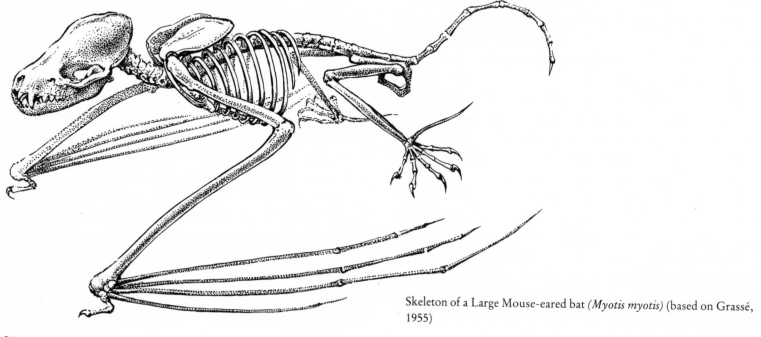

Skeleton of a Large Mouse-eared bat (*Myotis myotis*) (based on Grassé, 1955)

The development of sucker discs on the wrists and ankles of American Disc-winged bats (Thyropteridae). The discs produce a sticky secretion and have muscles that allow them to function as suckers. Adhesion is so effective that a single disc can support the entire weight of the bat (from Yalden and Morris, 1976).

The flight capacity of bats dominates every aspect of their life. It is the essential pre-requisite to obtaining food, and enables them to cover great distances between roost and feeding area. It is remarkable how particular kinds of food specializations are reflected in the adaptations of the organ of flight. Each species has developed the style of flight most appropriate to the requirements of its own way of life.

In the Megachiroptera, the wings are primarily a means of transportation from the roost to trees in feeding grounds many kilometres away. Therefore the demands made on them are quite different from those in species which require, for instance, a high degree of manoeuvrability in order to catch insects in flight. In avoiding obstacles or pursuing their prey, many species of bats show an agility which can be matched by few species of birds.

Body size and wing area are closely linked. A large, heavy body—and this is true of all flying animals—requires a larger lifting surface to support it in the air. Since, with an increase in the size of the animal by a given amount, the wing area increases by the square of this amount, while the volume, and therefore the weight, increases by the power of three, wing loading becomes increasingly heavy. But at a certain point, the animals reach a limit in body size beyond which flight is not possible. Among birds there are species incapable of flight —these are the cursorial birds such as the ostrich— whose bodies have attained a size which precludes the possibility of flight. No parallels exist among bats. There is no species with a body size which prevents it from flying.

The large Flying Foxes represent the limit of potential expansion of the wing area. This size of wing permits a slow but steady flight which is quite adequate for the bats as they move from place to place. More rapid and agile hunting flight such as is shown by many species of insectivorous bats is not possible with these large wings.

Flight in bats can be described as rowing flight. Many species have also mastered hovering flight such as is seen in raptors and humming-birds. Keeping the body erect, they are able to remain stationary in mid-air, without forward motion, like a helicopter. In this way, they can extract nectar from blossoms or pick insects off leaves.

Rowing flight can occasionally merge into a brief gliding flight. Extended periods of gliding, or soaring flight, is unknown among bats. The individual phases of move-

27

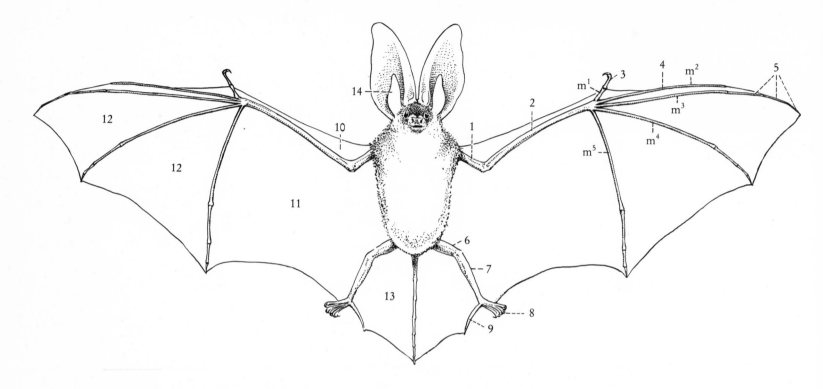

Diagram of the flight organ of a bat; supporting structures and the components of the membrane:
1 upper arm, 2 forearm, 3 thumb, 4 metacarpal bones (m^2, m^3, m^4, m^5), 5 digits, 6 upper leg, 7 lower leg, 8 hind foot, 9 calcar, 10 forward membrane (propatagium), 11 arm membrane (plagiopatagium), 12 finger membrane (chiropatagium or dactylopatagium), 13 tail or interfemoral membrane (uropatagium), 14 tragus or ear shield

ment in the course of a wing beat in rowing flight can be seen in the sketches on page 61. At the start of the down-stroke, the wing is directed backwards and upwards, with the tips of the wings behind the body's centre of gravity. Then the wings are swung outwards and downwards and after this, drawn forwards. At the lowest position of the wing stroke, the tips of the wings are a long way in front of the head. In this phase, the edges of the wings are drawn downwards, so that the wings have the shape of an open umbrella. The upstroke is not exactly the reverse movement, but now the wings are moved first upwards and then backwards. If one were able to mark out the track of the wing tip, it would—in relation to the body—describe an ellipse. In order to reduce air resistance during the upward stroke, many insectivorous bats fold the wings somewhat; the fruit bats raise them tightly folded past the sides of the body. The downbeat of the wing is a very important element of flight; it achieves both thrust and lift.

The number of wing beats per unit of time, that is the frequency of stroke, is much higher for insectivorous than for fruit bats. Large Mouse-eared bats raise and lower the wings an average of 11 to 12 times per second, and Lesser Horseshoe bats as many as 16 to 18 times. Only seven wing beats per second are reported for the fruit bat *Eidolon* sp. With this small number of strokes, the large fruit bats reach the same speed on an open stretch as most small insectivorous bats.

It has already been pointed out that the total extent of wing area has a significant effect on flight capacity. If the wing area is small in proportion to body size, loading is high and the stalling speed is increased. At first, the

animals are able to compensate for this by increasing the stroke frequency. But this is possible only to a limited extent, as it in turn depends upon the functional capacity of the flight muscles. The only solution is an enlargement of the wing area. It is interesting that among the suborder Microchiroptera, increase of the wing area always lags a little behind that of body size, while in the Megachiroptera, the size of the wing area runs ahead of that of the body. This is associated with the fact that among fruit bats, it has been possible for certain species to evolve which are larger than any of the insectivorous bats. This in turn has meant that the large species of fruit bats have a much lower stalling speed and can manage with a slower wing beat. Of course, such large wings, reaching spans of up to 2.00 m, are much more cumbersome since they meet with considerably greater air resistance than do wings of small area. Flight appears slow and ponderous. From a biological point of view, these wings fulfil all the demands made upon them by the fruit bat. It is not unusual for them to carry the bat a distance of 50 to 80 kilometres in one night from sleeping quarters to feeding area.

Among insectivorous bats there are few species that cover very long distances at night in search of food. The hunting territory of many Molossid bats, such as the Mexican Free-tailed bat (the Guano bat, *Tadarida brasiliensis*) which lives in millions in caves in the southern states of the U.S.A., may have a radius of about 75 kilometres. To make it possible for these vast numbers of bats to obtain sufficient food on their nocturnal flights, they are forced to cover distances of this order. But they are exceptional.

For most of the insectivorous bats, the capture of prey and the nature of the habitat within which the hunting is carried out calls for great flying skill. Within woodlands, the bat must alter direction with lightning speed and

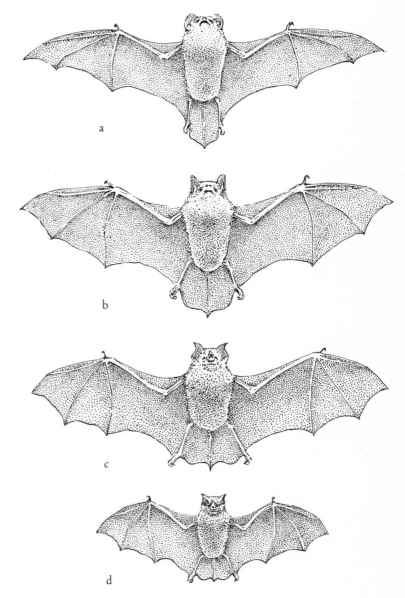

Silhouette of wing shapes of various bats
a Common Noctule *(Nyctalus noctula)*,
b Large Mouse-eared bat *(Myotis myotis)*,
c Greater Horseshoe bat *(Rhinolophus ferrumequinum)*,
d Lesser Horseshoe bat *(Rhinolophus hipposideros)*.
Characteristic of rapid hunting flight are long, narrow wings such as those of the Noctule. Broad wings such as those of the Lesser Horseshoe bat allow only slow but dexterous flight (after Gaisler, from Natuschke, 1960).

Diagram showing wing flight patterns for the Long-eared bat (*Plecotus* sp.) in hovering flight. The first 7 pictures show the downward movement of the wing (from Norberg, 1976).

great agility to avoid the many obstacles in its path. These requirements are best met by a short broad wing which also allows for hovering flight. On open ground, however, a greater wing area and a longer wing are advantageous. The bat can fly rapidly, catch food over a large area and escape from enemies more readily. A long, narrow wing is also found in those species of bats which cover long distances between their summer and winter roosts. Modifications in wing form and area occur primarily in the region of the hand membrane. There is also great variation in uropatagium associated with variation in leg, calcar and tail length. Few statistics exist for the speed of flight in bats, since it is a difficult measurement to make. For the Big Brown bat *(Eptesicus fuscus)* which is widely distributed in the U.S.A., speeds of up to 75 kilometres an hour are claimed. The Long-winged bat *(Miniopterus schreibersi)*, with 70 kilometres an hour, is said to be the fastest flying species in Europe. A speed of 50 kilometres per hour is given for the Common Noctule *(Nyctalus noctula)*. The Large Mouse-eared bat *(Myotis myotis)*, on the other hand, maintains a more leisurely stroke and covers only 15 kilometres in an hour. It is reported that fruit bats reach speeds of 15 to 30 kilometres an hour.

The tail membrane has little influence on the capability for flight. This can be deduced from the fact that it shows such great variation in the Microchiroptera, and is completely absent in a number of species. When present, it is

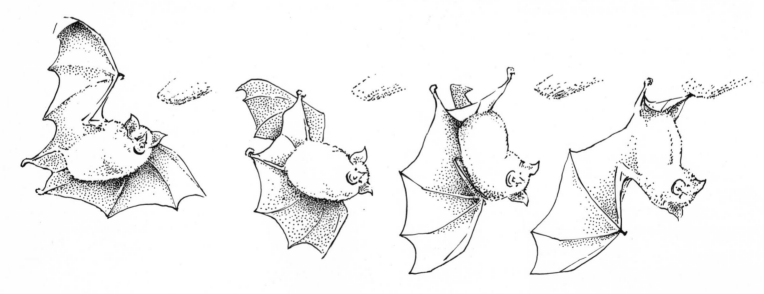

curved in flight and is used less for steering than for reducing the speed of flight when the bat is landing. The landing manoeuvre of bats at small projections on a wall or on rough wooden beams is quite an acrobatic feat. The finer points of landing technique differ from species to species. But all of them twist with a stroke of the wing away from the resting place on which they want to hang, in such a way that the feet can swing upwards and the talons immediately gain a firm hold. Although the widely spread wings slow down the descent like a parachute, the impetus of flight sometimes sends the bat hurtling downwards, particularly if the surface is very smooth, and then it must make another attempt.

Many fruit bats, on the other hand, land with the belly on the branches of their tree roosts. Then the claws of the hind feet and of the thumb seize branches and twigs and the bat takes up its roosting position.

In many species of the Microchiroptera, the tail membrane has taken on an additional function: it serves as a pouch when prey is being caught.

Flight demands a great expenditure of energy. The muscles of flight alone need an enormous supply of oxygen. In order to meet fuel requirements which in flight are four times greater than at rest, considerable demands are made on the organs of respiration and circulation. The high loading brought about during flight causes a massive increase in the cardiac and respiration rates. For

Diagram showing the landing manoeuvre of a Greater Horseshoe bat *(Rhinolophus ferrumequinum)*. In the last phase of approach to the wall or branch, the bat rolls to the right, round the axis of its own body, and lowering the body, it seizes hold with one foot. The extended wings check the momentum and the second foot seizes hold. The manoeuvre lasts about 110 milliseconds (from photographs by Kulzer and Weigold, 1978).

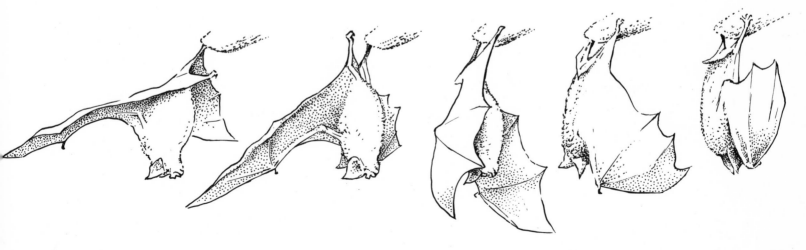

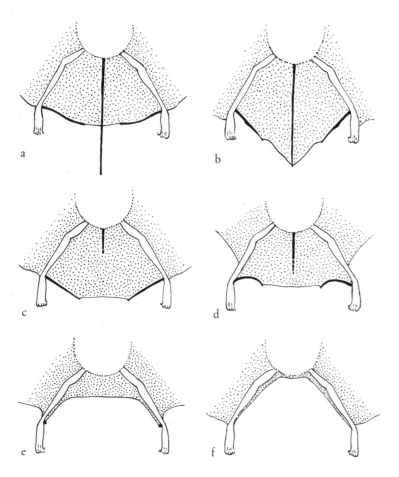

Differences in development of the tail and tail membrane (from Husson, 1962)

a *Eumops geijskesi* (Molossidae)
b *Lasiurus borealis* (Vespertilionidae)
c *Pteropteryx kappleri* (Emballonuridae)
d *Chilonycteris rubiginosa* (Chilonycteridae)
e *Desmodus rotundus* (Desmodontidae)
f *Sturnira lilium* (Phyllostomidae)

example, in the Spear-nosed bat *(Phyllostomus hastatus)*, the cardiac rate increases from 522 beats per minute at rest to 822 per minute in flight. Respiration rate increases from 180 to 560 per minute. The heart is considerably larger than in other mammals of the same size, and therefore is able to pump a much greater volume of blood through the body in the same length of time. In the blood, oxygen is carried to the muscles. Here, in comparison with other mammals, there is another difference. Whereas in the majority, the capacity of the blood to absorb oxygen is only 18 per cent by volume, in bats it reaches 27.

Physical work creates heat, and humans sweat. Bats are not able to maintain as constant a body temperature as, for example, carnivores or apes, so their temperature rises in flight. Unlimited, this could prove dangerous. After a maximum temperature is reached, bats benefit from a useful cooling system which, to some extent, helps to keep temperatures at a constant level. When body temperature rises, the small blood vessels within the membranes dilate and the increased quantities of blood flowing through are cooled by the cold stream of air passing the wings.

The structure of the bat's body shows various adaptations to flight. The neck is short, the chest is massive on account of the powerfully developed thoracic muscles. The adjoining abdomen is narrow and tapering. There are many other special biological features that are the consequence of the bat's power of flight, and which will be mentioned in other chapters of this book.

Distribution of bats throughout the world

For land mammals, the shoreline of the oceans and quite often great lakes and rivers represent significant obstacles which normally they are unable to cross. Bats, on the other hand, are able to cross at least lakes and rivers with no difficulty. Crossing oceans, however, is rarely within their capability. But since many species are capable of covering fifty kilometres and more in continuous flight, they are able to negotiate broad arms of the sea and to reach distant islands.

One example which shows that bats are often the first mammals to colonize an island is that of the island of Krakatau in the straits between Sumatra and Java. It lies 40 kilometres from the mainland and 18 from the closest neighbouring island. In a volcanic eruption in 1883, parts of the island were submerged and the rest buried beneath a shower of ash. All animal and plant life was destroyed. But the seemingly dead island did not keep its desolate appearance for long. Within three years it was green again as a new carpet of vegetation spread over it.

Man deliberately refrained from interfering and it was possible for detailed studies to be carried out on the natural process of recolonization by plants and animals. After 25 years, it could be shown that the animals which had gained a foothold there included 240 species of insects, 16 of birds and 2 of reptiles. After 37 years, there were more than 500 different species of animals including two species of bats as the first mammals.

The bat's capacity for flight is undoubtedly the reason why, in its 50 million years of existence on earth, the great army of bats has succeeded in extending its territory across every continent and to many islands.

Today they show a variety of form which is much greater in wealth of species in the tropics and subtropics than elsewhere. In both the northern and southern latitudes, as the distance from the equator increases, the number of species decreases very rapidly. It is logical therefore to look for centres of differentiation and speciation in the tropics.

The total number of species of bat found in Europe is 30; north of the Alps there are only 20 species, that is, not even 5 per cent of all species living in the world today. Apart from the temperature, it is food supply which more than any other factor presents the bats of the northern latitudes—they are all insectivores—with difficulties unknown to the tropical forms. They have adapted to the cold winters when food is scarce by hibernating during this critical period.

It is surprising to find that although all bats are capable of flight, there are certain families that occur on every continent, while others live only on one particular island. One inevitably asks: why do we find members of the suborder Megachiroptera—the fruit bats—in Asia and Africa, whereas the numerous family of Spear-nosed bats (Phyllostomidae) is encountered only in America?

In addition to temperature and food supply, another important factor in determining the distribution of bats was the displacement of continental land masses that took place long ago in geological history. Another point perhaps of considerable significance in answering these questions is that in spite of the ability to fly, not all species show equally strong migratory tendencies. Newly evolved species did not begin immediately to disperse over a wider area. Often the specific environment of a region or island and perhaps a certain food that was available suited them well, and they remained in that particular locality. In other cases, if the situation was less favourable, the creatures moved across country and settled in new areas. Millions of years ago, land masses drifted apart and land bridges were severed, so that individual populations were separated from their place of origin, and over thousands of years, they underwent changes. New species evolved. This is why islands such as Borneo, Java and Madagascar possess such an independent fauna. Of the species living today, there are some which occur in several continents. Interestingly enough, they are always found in similar biotopes; even at the opposite ends of their area of distribution, these species inhabit the same type of living quarters or the same landscape.

This constancy in respect of environment shown by individual species can be used to detect changes in our environment. The arrival of new species, or—as is much more common in Europe—their disappearance, are certain signs of such change.

If we consider the families of bats living in the world today from the point of view of their distribution, we can distinguish three major groups:
1) those living exclusively on the continents and islands of the Old World (nine families);
2) those occurring only in the New World (six families);
3) those which are found both in the Old and the New World (three families).
Among the nine Old World families, there are three which are represented by only a single species. These are the Short-tailed bats (Mystacinidae) which exist in New Zealand, the Sucker-footed bats (Myzopodidae) found only in Madagascar and the Hog-faced bats (Craseonycteridae) found only in Thailand. The typical feature distinguishing members of the second family is the presence of suction discs on the feet and the balls of the thumb. Quite independent of the Madagascan Sucker-footed bats, suction pads of this kind have also been developed by the two species of the family of American Disc-winged bats (Thyropteridae) living in tropical South America. This is a good example of convergent evolution within the animal kingdom, which in no way implies close relationships.

The six remaining families which inhabit only the eastern hemisphere are concentrated mainly in the tropics and subtropics. The many species of Megachiroptera make up a single family, the fruit bats or Flying Foxes (Pteropodidae). They live in India, Southeast Asia, Africa and the northern part of Australia. The distribution of the true Flying Foxes (Pteropus spp.) is of particular zoogeographical interest, for although they are absent from the African mainland, they are found on the small island of Pemba which lies only 60 kilometres off the east coast of Africa, and Mafia, 16 kilometres from the same coast. It is not clear how the creatures got here, particularly since they are closer to the species living in the Malayan regions than to the Flying Foxes of India and Sri Lanka. Could it be that a storm cast them up like flotsam off the coast of Africa, or even that their ancestors lived on the African mainland? In any case, other fruit-eating Megachiroptera, usually smaller species, are found today only in Equatorial and South Africa.

The distribution of the Slit-faced bats (Nycteridae) of the suborder Microchiroptera suggests that continuous forests once extended from the Congo to Indonesia. Members of the family are found particularly in the primeval forests of Africa. They are entirely absent from the Indian region, yet they are found again in Southeast Asia. Early authors described the members of this family as wholly forest-dwelling. More recent observations have shown that they also extend into steppe regions, and certain species have become indigenous there.

The many species of the family of Horseshoe bats (Rhinolophidae) are found primarily in tropical regions. Their area of distribution extends from Africa across India, southern China and as far as the East Indies. But they are absent from both Madagascar and various islands of the Indo-Australian archipelago. Certain species of this family are found in temperate latitudes. As relics of warmer days, the fauna of central Europe still includes the Greater Horseshoe bat (Rhinolophus ferrum-

equinum) and the Lesser Horseshoe bat *(Rhinolophus hipposideros)*. Unfortunately, the Greater Horseshoe bat has become quite a rarity north of the Alps, and in recent years, an alarming decline in the numbers of Lesser Horseshoe bats has been reported. In Europe today they are numbered among the endangered species. The Old World Leaf-nosed bats of the family Hipposideridae, which also contains many species, are closely related to the Rhinolophidae. Their area of distribution coincides almost exactly with that of the latter, except that since they are unable to hibernate, members of this family are not found in temperate latitudes.

The small number of species in the families of Mouse-tailed bats (Rhinopomatidae) and False Vampires or "cannibal bats" (Megadermatidae) are today exclusively tropical forms. Fossil finds of Megadermatids from the Oligocene and the Miocene show that this family—and doubtless others as well—was also widespread in Europe millions of years ago.

Six families of bats occur exclusively in the New World. The majority of them live in tropical and subtropical regions. The greatest variety of forms, which is reflected in a large number of species, has been developed by the Spear-nosed bats (Phyllostomidae). It has been assumed that this family developed and achieved its high degree of differentiation in South America. Only very few species, in the northernmost extent of their range, reach the south-west of the U.S.A.

Purely tropical forms are the blood-feeding Vampire bats (Desmodontidae), which are probably descended from Spear-nosed bats. They live in an area which extends from southern Mexico to Brazil.

Another group of specialized feeders among the Chiroptera of the New World which has approximately the same area of distribution is the family of Fisherman bats (Noctilionidae).

Area of distribution of Vampire bats (Desmodontidae) in Central and South America (after Greenhall, 1975)

A parallel to the distribution of various species of Old World fruit-eating bats that occur only on particular islands in the East Indies is provided in the New World by the Funnel-eared bats (Natalidae). Many species of this family are found only on a few islands in the West Indies.

Of the three families with species occurring both in the Old and the New World, the Sheath-tailed bats (Emballonuridae) and the Free-tailed bats (Molossidae) are restricted in their distribution to the tropics and subtropics. Representatives of these families can be found in sites at opposite ends of the earth, thousands of miles apart. A comparison in terms of morphological and ecological specialization of bats of different genera that are indigenous to either Africa or South America, shows interesting similarities. It is tempting to conclude from these that the species of the New World derive from those of the Old. But this is not justified, since the similarities result rather from parallel developments that have taken place in like

39

but widely separated biotopes. Nevertheless, the genera have indeed a common ancestral stock. But that dates far back in the history of the world.

Among the Molossidae, only a few species live in the warmer regions of the temperate zone. The Free-tailed bat *Tadarida teniotis* is found today in Spain, Italy and Greece. Other species of this genus extend into the southern states of the U.S.A. Best known of all is the Guano bat, *Tadarida brasiliensis*, which spends the summer in caves, roosting in its millions.

About a quarter of the 320 species of Vespertilionid bats (sometimes called Vesper bats; Vespertilionidae) are not restricted in their distribution to the warm regions of the earth, but also inhabit temperate zones. Most of the bats of Europe, North America and Japan belong to this family. They are also found on many islands in the Pacific and the Atlantic (Bermudas, Azores, Galápagos, Hawaii).

Numerous morphological features together with the fact that they are insectivorous suggest that many species of this family are very primitive forms. Since they have not developed a high degree of specialization, it has been possible for members of this family to adapt easily, compared to others, and to occupy niches in which specialized species would be incapable of survival. For example, we find members of the genus *Myotis* (Mouse-eared bats) in the most northerly regions of the eastern and western hemispheres. They have extended the scope of their distribution to the northern limit of tree growth between Norway and Kamchatka, and are also found on the Alaskan and Labrador peninsulas. The Little Brown bat *(Myotis lucifugus)* is distributed across the whole of North America. Closely related species inhabit Central and South America as far as Chile and Argentina. In the Old World, the Daubenton's or Water bat *(Myotis daubentoni)* extends its range from Western Europe across Northern Asia to the Pacific coast. Some members of the large genera of Pipistrelles *(Pipistrellus)* and Big Brown bats *(Eptesicus)* are similarly very widely distributed, although the northern limits of their range do not extend as far as those of the Mouse-eared bats. It is known from the evidence of fossil plants and animals that some 50 million years ago, average temperatures in Europe were much higher than they are today; consequently the spectrum of Vespertilionids was much wider. In addition, many more species from other families—even Flying Foxes—were found here. The decline in temperature which reached its peak during the glacial period forced a great many of the warmth-loving species to retreat into areas where conditions suited them better. There was a great reduction in species in temperate latitudes.

It is interesting to take a look at Australia, an island continent with a highly specialized mammalian fauna. Anyone who considers only the egg-laying mammals or the many marsupials may be led to assume that this is an oasis for the earliest and most primitive mammals. But a glance at the bat fauna gives a very different picture. There are only a few very old "endemic" species, such as the Tube-nosed Fruit bats (Nyctimeninae). Much more common are quite "modern" representatives of Chiroptera that occur on the neighbouring islands of Southeast Asia. The cosmopolitan genera *Myotis*, *Pipistrellus* and *Eptesicus* are also represented in Australia.

Many species of bats only established themselves in Australia considerably later than the primitive population of mammals such as the spiny anteater, duck-billed platypus and the marsupials. The sea channels between the islands proved no barrier to the expansion of the Indo-Malayan bat fauna into the Australian region. The result is that, in contrast to other groups of mammals, fewer differences exist between the bat fauna of Australia and the rest of the Old World than between the bat fauna of the Old World and the Americas.

17 Epauletted Fruit bats
(*Epomophorus anurus*; Pteropodidae). These bats rest with
their wing membranes folded
round them, as if in a protective
blanket.

42

18   Zenker's Fruit bats (*Scoto-nycteris zenkeri*; Pteropodidae). These small representatives of the Epauletted Fruit bats lack the usual hair tufts on the shoulder. They reach a body length of 8 cm and a wing span of 30 cm.

19 Tube-nosed Fruit bat (*Nyctimene* sp.; Pteropodidae). So called because they have extended tubular nostrils.

20 Wahlberg's Epauletted Fruit bat (*Epomophorus wahlbergi*; Pteropodidae). The shoulder pouches of these bats are surrounded by tufts of light-coloured hair (epaulettes). The white hairs on the front and back edge of the ear are typical of this species.

21 Dwarf Long-tongued Fruit bat (*Macroglossus minimus*; Pteropodidae). These bats are among the smallest of the fruit bats, up to 7 cm in length of body, with a wing span of 25 cm. The elongated head indicates specialization in nectar feeding.

22 *Rousettus stresemanni*
(Pteropodidae); one of the cave-
dwelling fruit bats

23   Indian Flying Fox *(Pteropus giganteus)* engaged in grooming

24   The Hammer-headed Fruit bat (*Hypsignathus monstrosus*; Pteropodidae). The largest species of fruit bat in Africa. The hammer-shaped muzzle of this bat carries pendulous mouth lappets. The males of the species are larger than the females (body length up to 20 cm); the wing span is 90 cm.

Fruit bats (Megachiroptera)— an Old World family of bats with many species

In what way do they differ from the Microchiroptera?

The Megachiroptera (great bats) is the name used to denote the suborder of fruit bats ("flying foxes"), consisting of about 175 species. The name was chosen when only the large species of Flying Foxes were known. A look at the members of the suborder today shows that the name is a misleading one. The largest of the bats are indeed found among the Flying Foxes, but there are also certain small species in the suborder which are exceeded in size by some of the Microchiroptera.

If it is not size, is it perhaps choice of diet which distinguishes the Megachiroptera from the Microchiroptera? In older literature, they were described as the fruit eaters in contrast to the Microchiroptera that were assumed to be purely insectivorous. But neither is this distinction a valid one. It has long since been established that some of the Microchiroptera are also fruit-eating species.

What then are the differences? There are certain anatomical features that justify the division of bats into two major suborders. Of these, an important one is the presence, exclusive to the Megachiroptera, of a small claw on the second digit. This feature alone is not sufficient to make the distinction in every case, since members of the Bare-backed fruit bats (*Dobsonia* sp.) and a few other groups possess no claw on the second digit.

Another feature typical of although not exclusive to fruit bats is the reduction of the caudal vertebrae and, as a result, the absence of an externally visible tail. In only very few species is there a fully developed tail similar to that of the fossil bat *Archaeopteropus*. On the other hand, reduction of the tail is also found among the Microchiroptera, particularly in certain of the fruit-eating Spearnosed bats of the New World. As a result of this feature, most fruit-eating bats have no tail membrane or only a rudimentary one that can be seen as a narrow fold of skin on the inside of the lower leg. Thus, no single feature but a series of features makes it possible to decide whether a species is assignable to the Megachiroptera or not.

In spite of their nocturnal habit, fruit bats on the whole navigate by means of visual perception. For this purpose, like the nocturnally active owl, they have comparatively large eyes. Orientation by means of echolocation which the Microchiroptera master to perfection has not been evolved by the Megachiroptera. There is one exception: fruit bats of the genera *Rousettus* and *Lissonycteris* are capable of both optical and acoustical orientation by means of echolocation.

Examination of the eyes of fruit bats has shown that they are extremely well adapted for nocturnal vision. Two features possessed by the eyes of other mammals are not found in those of fruit bats, since they are unimportant for nocturnal vision; firstly, fruit bats lack the ability to distinguish colour and secondly, they are unable to alternate between near and distant vision. The lens of the eye is particularly thick and thus achieves a high refractive power. In this way, only small but very intense images are produced on the retina. In addition, the number of light-sensitive receptors in the retina of the fruit bat is very great, exceeding those in the eye of the owl. Experiments have shown that the enhanced efficiency of the fruit bat's eye takes the form of a greatly improved sharpness of vision even in semi-darkness. On their nocturnal flights in search of food, the creatures show great skill in avoiding obstacles and reaching their feeding places safely.

The sense of smell plays an important part in the location of food. A sensitive nose is an undoubted asset in detecting the aromatic scent of ripe fruit in darkness. Experiments have shown Rousette Fruit bats to be capable of locating small pieces of banana only 10 mg in weight that were hidden in their cage. The creatures could also distinguish easily between the smell of real bananas and a chemically produced aroma. Examination of the brain of the fruit bat has also shown that the sense of vision and the sense of smell are of vital importance to fruit bats in establishing contact with the environment and particularly in finding food. The brain centres associated with particular sense organs clearly reflect in their degree of development and differentiation, differences in the functional efficiency of those sense organs. Quantitative analyses of the appropriate brain centres have shown that in the case of fruit bats, not only the olfactory centre of the brain but also and to an even greater extent the optical centres are much more highly developed than they are in insectivorous bats. Conversely, the acoustic centres in the brain of fruit bats show only slight or, more accurately, normal development.

Extensive analyses of the size of the brain or separate parts of the brain of numerous species of bats carried out in recent years have called into question the widely accepted assumption that the Megachiroptera are more primitive than the Microchiroptera. In assessing the level of development in bats, emphasis was always laid on the degree of refinement achieved in the development of flight, that is, on a feature of specialization. Up to now, little consideration has been given to the extent of brain development, that is, to centralization. Research carried out by the Frankfurt brain specialist Stephan showed that there is considerable variation in the development of the brains of individual species of bats. There is a close correlation between diet and the degree of brain specialization, quite independent of the family to which the species belongs. The fruit bats are something of an exception. On the basis of measurements made of the neocortex, they are found to have achieved the highest degree of brain development among bats. The neocortex is four to five times larger than that of primitive insectivorous species. In this respect, the fruit bats are surpassed only by the highly specialized Vampires and the fish-eating bats.

Giants and dwarfs among the Megachiroptera

The great variation in body size that can occur among different species of fruit bats is illustrated in the contrast between certain bats with a body weight of 1000 g and others weighing only 5 g. Wing spread varies accordingly, ranging from 200 cm to 25 cm.

Apart from differences in size, most species of fruit bats are fairly similar in appearance. Striking facial appendages are usually absent. Only the Australasian Tube-nosed bat (*Nyctimene* sp.) and the Hammer-headed or Horse-faced Fruit bat (*Hypsignathus monstrosus*) of Africa, with its grotesque muzzle, deviate from the general pattern. Adaptation to the nectar-feeding habit has produced in some species a long narrow snout rather different in appearance from the usual fox-like or dog-like head of the Megachiroptera.

Since bats in zoos do not have the same appeal to the public as, for instance, monkeys, nor are they easy to look after, there is very little opportunity to get to know them in captivity. Those few bats that are kept, however, are usually large species of flying foxes belonging to the true Fruit bats (Pteropodinae).

The largest African representative of this group is the grey to reddish-brown Straw-coloured bat (*Eidolon helvum*), which measures 20 cm from head to rump. These creatures are very gregarious and, during the day, assemble in large communal roosts on high trees. Roosts of this kind are sometimes found in the centre of large towns, where even heavy traffic fails to disturb these otherwise timid creatures. In a large gathering of this kind, it is striking to see how the individual animals carry out certain activities such as grooming almost simultaneously.

After sunset, the *Eidolon* roosting communities become active and prepare to fly off towards the trees where they feed. The general departure is accompanied by a good deal of clamour as wing membranes are once again thoroughly cleaned and groomed. Then the bats fly off quietly in small groups. On the way, they visit watering places at which they quench their thirst. To drink, the bats fly low over the surface of the water, and in flight, scoop up water with the mouth. They eat noisily throughout the night. In doing so, they often maintain a hold on a branch with only one foot, while with the other they grip the fruit, pressing it against the chest and biting pieces from it. They spit out hard parts and fibrous matter, which fall to the ground. Feeding is by no means a peaceful process. Fruit bats are voracious feeders, and fighting for the best places with the ripest fruits is accompanied by a constant screeching and fluttering. At intervals, they rest and fly to other trees in the vicinity to feed. Only with the break of day do the bats return to their roosts on trees that are often many kilometres away. Even here they do not immediately fall quiet. Grooming is carried out and there are hours of noisy quarrelling over the best roosting places until the community eventually settles to sleep.

Although most fruit bats roost on trees, members of the genera *Rousettus, Eonycteris, Notopteris* and *Lissonycteris* roost in caves. They are medium-sized species which are found in the tropical regions of the Old World. They do not occur in Australia. Little is known of the habits of most of the species since they are active at night and it is difficult to observe them in their natural habitats.

Probably more is known about the habits of the Egyptian Fruit bat (*Rousettus aegyptiacus)* than of any other. In recent years, this species has been the subject of detailed investigation, and for this purpose has frequently been kept in laboratories.

The Egyptian Fruit bats, the distribution of which extends into the Mediterranean area as far as Cyprus, also live in large assemblies, spending the day in tombs, caves and the cellars of old buildings. Their sleep is not a deep one, and the slightest noise wakens them. At any disturbance, the creatures retreat into any chinks and crevices they can find. After dark, they leave their gloomy quarters and fly to the trees on which they feed. On light nights, they can be seen in towns among avenues of trees, if these provide the food they require. At first, they hover over the fruit to examine its scent before landing on the tree. Here they clamber about, using their keen sense of smell to lead them to the ripest fruits. Feeding is followed by an extensive period of grooming, in which fur and wing membranes are licked clean and fragments of food removed from the claws of the thumbs and feet using the teeth. Since these species—and the cave-dwelling Angola Fruit bat (*Lissonycteris angolensis)* to an equal extent —are known to use ultrasonic orientation in addition to having eyes with highly efficient nocturnal vision, they are able to inhabit dark recesses of caves where no light penetrates. In this darkness, they are able to find their way by means of their "radar system". The sounds emitted by *Rousettus* are produced not by the larynx as in the Microchiroptera, but by the tongue. As soon as the bats approach the lighter entrance to the cave, they change over from the acoustical to the optical system of orientation. This optimal development of two sense organs as important for orientation as ear and eye, has enabled this group of fruits bats to colonize habitats which remain unavailable to most other species.

The daily alternation of light-dark, or day-night, provides the stimulus for the phases of rest and activity. When the bats are hanging from trees, they have no difficulty in determining the onset of dusk. But how do cave dwellers know when it is getting dark and the time is near to set out after food? Experiments have shown that in addition to the direct effect of light, a kind of "internal clock" helps to determine the daily routine. Towards evening it stimulates the cave-dwelling bats. They fly to the cave entrance to check external conditions of darkness. If it is still too light, departure is delayed. Experiments in which the dark phase of the day was reduced to two hours, had the interesting effect of reducing the activity phase to this length as well. For the Egyptian Fruit bat in particular, the periodic unit of the internal clock is approximately 24 hours. In this way, the bat is so well adapted to the passage of the natural day that it always wakens at the correct time. Combined with ultrasonic orientation, this periodicity is a supplementary and very useful adaptation to nocturnal activity and life in caves.

In their day-time roost, the mass assemblies of fruit bats usually include males, females and, in the appropriate season, young animals. Purely female colonies, such as are known to exist in many species of Microchiroptera in the form of maternity colonies have scarcely been observed among fruit bats. However, Eisentraut reports that on his journeys through Cameroon, he came across assemblies of Angola Fruit bats in various caves, which consisted entirely of females. The animals were hanging close together from the roofs of caves and were in late stages of pregnancy or had already borne young. So the possibility cannot be ruled out that some species of fruit bats also set up maternity groups.

Among fruit bats, the genus *Pteropus* which is found from islands of extreme western Indian Ocean through Southeast Asia to Australia and in many of the islands of the South Pacific, contains the largest number of species including those known as Flying Foxes. Many of them have a very strictly limited area of distribution. In many cases, each island has its own particular species. One of the largest species is the Flying Fox of India *Pteropus giganteus*, which is light to dark brown in colouring and has a wing span of 120 cm. While its home is principally India and Sri Lanka as well as the slopes of the Himalayas, its larger relation, the Kalong (*Pteropus vampyrus*) inhabits the Malayan Peninsula and the islands of Indonesia and the Philippines. A giant among the Flying Foxes is the Javanese Kalong with a body length of 40 cm and a wing spread of 170 cm. In comparison, the Grey-headed Flying Fox (*Pteropus poliocephalus*) from the eastern coastal regions of Australia, with a wing span of only 100 cm, and the Rufous Flying Fox (*Pteropus rufus*) found on Madagascar, with about the same dimensions, seem moderately small creatures.

The large species of Flying Foxes of Asia and Australia also spend the day sleeping in roosting colonies or "camps". Often they seek out very tall trees, which can even be in the middle of towns or villages. Like the Microchiroptera, they remain faithful to their roosting sites, sometimes for several generations. As a result of constant colonization, the trees are partly or entirely denuded of foliage. It is an impressive sight for the traveller who comes upon a "classic" colony of this kind with thousands of bats hanging like pendulous fruit from the branches of trees. Each animal can be distinguished separately, for in spite of their gregarious nature, they avoid any physical contact and are careful to maintain a certain distance between themselves and their neighbours, in order to sleep undisturbed.

In these roosts, the hundreds or even thousands of bats are exposed to all weathers. Since the branches from which they hang are often bare, the bats have to endure the full heat of the sun as well as storm and rain. In addition, they must compensate for seasonal fluctuations in temperature in the different biotopes.

Diagram showing wing flight patterns for the fruit bat *Eidolon helvum*
a from in front, b from the side (from Kulzer, 1968)

The large wing membranes serve as a valuable means of protection. In the full heat of the midday sun, the bats are usually wide awake, and with extended wings, they waft cool air towards their body in a fanning action. They can also lose a lot of heat from their large, well-vasculated wing membranes. When it is cold and wet, the patagium is folded tightly round the body, providing good protection from the inclemencies of the weather.

The Tübingen physiologist Kulzer examined heat regulation in Flying Foxes under experimental conditions, and was able to confirm the pattern of behaviour shown by the bats in roosting communities. At temperatures of between 18°C and 30°C, the creatures hold their wings loosely folded against the body. If the temperature is raised, the bats spread out their wings and begin to fan themselves with cool air. It is dangerous and may easily be fatal if the normal body temperature is exceeded by only a few degrees. In the conditions described above, Flying Foxes are particularly susceptible to heatstroke. It is impressive to observe the way in which they protect themselves, even under experimental conditions. When the ambient temperature reaches 37°C and over, the animals make use of cooling by evaporation to dissipate excess heat. Since they are unable to sweat, they begin to lick their body and wing membranes extensively. They almost look as if they had been submerged in water. At the same time, they intensify the fanning action of the wings so that more cool air is brought into contact with the body. This increases evaporation, and the Flying Foxes achieve the same result as, for example, man and many animals do when they sweat. With a normal body temperature of about 37°C, Flying Foxes can tolerate an increase to 40°C or more for only a short time. As soon as these refrigerative measures cease to be effective, the creatures fly off. It can be assumed, that in natural conditions, Flying Foxes avoid dangerous overheating by leaving the roosting sites. Since bats are usually active only at night, additional heat generated by muscle activity, particularly in flight, is very important. The considerable drop in temperature at night in the tropics causes cooling of the body. This can be counterbalanced by the generation of additional heat in flying.

When the temperature of the environment was reduced in the experiments, it became essential for the animals to avoid any unnecessary loss of body warmth and to reduce to a minimum heat loss by radiation from the surface of the body. They wrapped themselves firmly in their wing membranes as in a cloak; head and nose and even one of the feet were all hidden beneath the patagium. In their natural habitat, the temperatures in the open never sink to freezing point, so the Flying Foxes are able in this way to maintain a constant body temperature even during cool periods. These findings are in direct contrast to those concerning the regulation of body temperature in insectivorous bats (Microchiroptera) in temperate regions. When temperatures are low, they enter a state of torpor which causes a considerable lowering of the body temperature. The experiments with Flying Foxes, however, suggest that most species of the Megachiroptera are true warm-blooded animals (homoiotherms).

In many mammals it is possible to distinguish the sexes by externally visible features. Secondary sexual characteristics of this kind are absent in many of the Chiroptera. Without close examination, it is not usually possible to tell male and female apart. Certain of the Flying Foxes, however, show sexual dimorphism. They include the group of Epauletted Fruit bats (*Epomops, Epomophorus*) living in the forests of Africa. The males of these species are usually rather larger than the females and in addition possess glandular pouches in the skin of the shoulder which are surrounded by light-coloured tufts of hair. These produce the effect of epaulettes. Little is known about the habits of these fruit bats. During the day, they remain concealed in small groups among bushes along the banks of streams in primitive forests, and are difficult to observe.

Included in this group of Epauletted bats, although lacking the tufts of hair on the shoulders, is the Hammer-headed or Horse-faced Fruit bat *(Hypsignathus monstrosus)*, which, with its massive head, has a monstrous and bizarre appearance. In this species, the males are much larger than the females. With a wing span of some 90 cm, they are giants among the African Flying Foxes. A striking feature of the ponderous head is the greatly swollen hammer-shaped muzzle. The pendulous lips are particularly suitable for enclosing whole fruits and squeezing the juice from them.

Eisentraut observed that at mating time, the males will spend hours at a time producing curious deep booming sounds. A much enlarged larynx is the structural basis for this vocal effect. Calls of this kind are otherwise virtually unknown among Chiroptera. It is very probable that, as in the case of many other animals, they serve a sexual purpose, helping to attract the female.

All the species mentioned so far belong to the Pteropodinae or Long-nosed Flying Foxes. They contrast with the subfamily of Short-nosed Fruit bats (Cynopterinae), the species of which live only in the Indo-Malayan region. Most of them are quite small forms with a wing spread of 30 to 45 cm. They are scarcely larger than our own indigenous bats. Most species live communally, roosting during the day on trees. In many areas they hang on branches of palm trees where they are well protected from sun and rain by the large leaves. Short-nosed Fruit bats have also been found in caves and hollow trees. In many places they live in human habitations.

The majority of the Short-nosed Fruit bats are fruit eaters. They have also been observed to visit blossoms.

But no special adaptation to this type of feeding is discernible. On the other hand, the members of the subfamily of Long-tongued Fruit bats (Macroglossinae) are exclusively nectar eating. These bats live in the Asiatic-Australian region and one species in Africa. They are small species, which with their narrow extended skull and long slender tongue are extremely well adapted to visiting blossoms. They are able to insert their long snout deep into a blossom and extract nectar or pollen with the tongue. The Macroglossinae include the smallest of the fruit bats. The Asiatic Long-tongued Fruit bat *(Macroglossus minimus)* has a body length of only 7 cm and a wing span of 25 cm. With these dimensions, it is considerably smaller than many of the Microchiroptera.

There is one group which stands out from the majority of fruit bats on account of curious external features. These are the Tube-nosed Fruit bats *(Nyctimene* sp.). As their name reflects, the nostrils of these species are prolonged as scroll-like tubes some 6 to 7 mm in length. These tubular nostrils lend the creatures a strange, somewhat eerie appearance. It is not known whether they have any functional significance. If the bats make use of any form of supersonic orientation—and it is not known that they do—the nasal tubes might possibly be linked with a particular kind of sound emission. In the case of many insectivorous bats, curious elaborations of the tissues of the face have proved to fulfil a vitally important function. In addition to this extraordinary nasal modification, the markings of the body are interesting, being of a kind rarely met with in bats. The Tube-nosed Fruit bats have a random distribution of yellow spots over the entire body and wing membranes. They stand out distinctly against the brown background of the creature's fur. This marking provides useful camouflage protection to the small animals as they hang suspended among foliage on trees during the day.

Nose and ears— distinguishing features of bats (Microchiroptera)

It is astonishing what an abundance of forms mammals have evolved in the course of millions of years, since their prototypes first appeared in the early Tertiary. The Microchiroptera in particular, that is, those known as "insectivorous" bats, illustrate this diversity with nearly 800 species. There is no doubt that the capacity for flight has been a significant factor in contributing to the development of variety within this group of mammals. Since they are able to fly and are active during the hours of night, bats have scarcely any enemies that pursue them. In the tropics of the Old World, it is the Bat-hawk *(Machaerhamphus alcinus)* and in those of the New World, the Bat-falcon *(Falco rufigularis)* that specialize in hunting bats. Certain other kinds of vertebrates will lie in wait at the entrance to a cave to catch a bat as it flies out in the evening. But on the whole, the ancestors of bats were able to evolve and specialize undisturbed, and over millions of years, to produce a great wealth of forms.

And yet a glance at the European species of bats may well produce the impression that they hardly vary at all from one another. Apart from the Horseshoe bats with their complex nose leaf, all other forms appear inconspicuous, with a "normal" shape of head and with only slight differences in body size, ear structure and colour of pelage. Even the expert sometimes finds it no easy task to distinguish between such similar pairs as the Common Pipistrelle and Nathusius' Pipistrelle, or the Grey Long-eared bat and the Brown Long-eared bat. So it is not surprising if, for most people, just as one mouse is like any other mouse, so one bat is like any other bat. It is rare to have the opportunity to see several species together at one time, since, to a large extent, they elude observation by their nocturnal, secretive habits.

Until recently, all that was known of many species, even to specialists, was the description and place of origin. A comparison of the numerous species of bat, however, shows that one bat is certainly not very much like every other. In the tropics in particular, a long process of evolution has produced some really exciting forms.

Of great diversity, and therefore an essential feature in distinguishing species, is the form of the head. In some species, the face has an appearance little short of grotesque. The fleshy nasal appendages found in many species show enormous variation. But their form is so characteristic that they have been responsible for the common names of some families, such as the Horseshoe, Spear-nosed, Leaf-nosed or Slit-faced bats. For most species, the significance of these appendages is not known. As will be shown in connection with echolocation, they certainly do not represent mere whims of nature, but may have a vitally important function. Like the nose leaf, the ears of many species are of exceptional dimensions and have a distinctly individual form. Even the tragus, a membranous lobe which projects at the front of the ear orifice, may be smooth or notched, broad or long, round or pointed. A third feature which can give the face a characteristic appearance is the form of the lips. They are not always smooth but may be indented or wrinkled and covered with wart-like growths. All these elements produce faces that can often seem grotesque or hideous in appearance.

The Microchiroptera are small forms with a body size in general smaller than that of most fruit bats. The smallest of them, *Craseonycteris thonglongyai*, was discovered in Thailand only some 10 years ago. The small size of this species (length of head and body 29 to 33 mm; weight 1.7 to 2.0 g) makes it the smallest living mammal. The largest species can reach 18 cm (the Giant Spear-nosed or Linné's False Vampire bat, *Vampyrum spectrum* of tropical America; the Australian False Vampire bat, *Macroderma gigas*). Among Microchiroptera, the wing spread ranges from 15 to 90 cm.

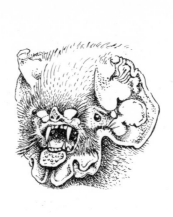
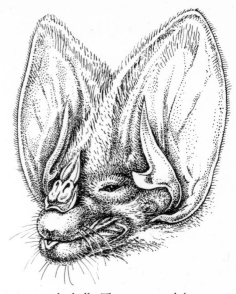

Face of the Leaf-chinned bat *Mormoops megalophylla*. The numerous lobes and folds near the ears and on the lower lip have earned it the name of the Wrinkle-faced bat.

This False Vampire (Megadermatidae) owes its popular name of Ghost bat to the shape of its head (from Felten, 1958).

A feature common to them all is the absence of a claw on the second digit. Most species have a well-developed tail with an interfemoral membrane developed accordingly. Among Spear-nosed bats there is some variation here; the tail and interfemoral membrane show various degrees of regression. As an adaptation to a very wide range of feeding habits, the teeth of bats are often reduced in number. In addition, the entire skull may be modified, varying from elongate to short with "pug-like" proportions. The fur covering usually does not extend to any part of the patagium, the ears and facial embellishments. A fact of interest to the bat systematist is that the individual hair shows typical structural features in its outer cortex. It may appear scaly like a fir cone or show transverse protruberances or a spiral thread. This surface conformation is often so specific that it can help to determine genera.

The fur of most bats is grey or brownish in colour, with varying gradations of lightness. Bright colours such as orange-red or rufous-brown are rare. The same is true of markings on the fur; only a few species show spots or stripes. Striking differences in colour in the skin of the body and of the patagium are found rarely. The markings of the East African species *Myotis welwitschi* are outstanding. The yellow colour of the fur, which is extended across the tail membrane, contrasts strongly with the mat black of the wing membranes. In the Microchiroptera, as in most Megachiroptera, colouration varies hardly at all between the sexes. Sometimes the females are rather more intensely coloured than the males, as for example, in the American Red bat *(Lasiurus borealis)*.

Although the Microchiroptera are distributed all over the world, they are nevertheless heat-loving animals, essentially requiring warmth, and are therefore encountered in very large numbers in the tropics and subtropics. But some species have extended their territory to the edge of the Arctic zone, stopping only where the insect food supply ceases. Those bats indigenous to Europe are representatives of the families of Vespertilionid bats (Vespertilionidae), Horseshoe bats (Rhinolophidae) and one species of Free-tailed bats (Molossidae). So vast is the number of species which comprise the seventeen families of the Microchiroptera that here we are able to consider only a few in detail, but they will probably suffice to illustrate the great diversity in form and habit.

Mouse-tailed bats (Rhinopomatidae)

This primitive family contains only 3 species and they differ somewhat from the generally accepted "typical" bat form. The long, thin tail has only a narrow edging of skin tissue at its root. Is the interfemoral membrane rudimentary, or are these species so primitive that they do not yet possess a tail membrane? The ears are large and are connected at the anterior base. The snout is naked and has an extended appearance; at the centre of the upper lip there is a rudimentary nose leaf.

Bats of this family are found round the Sahara region, and also in the Near East, India and Southeast Asia. They live communally in caves and old buildings, and are commonly found in ancient tombs in Egypt. Thick layers of droppings that have piled up beneath roosting places show that the colonies have inhabited the same quarters continuously for hundreds of years. Mouse-tailed bats are insectivorous and are found in very hot, arid regions. During cool periods and when food is scarce, the bats become torpid and live on subcutaneous reserves of fat that they have accumulated at the base of the tail.

Slit-faced bats (Nycteridae)

This family is also restricted to the Old World. Its representatives are distinguished by a particular structural feature of the skull; the nostrils lie within a deep hollow in the front of the skull that extends to the brow, and which is bordered by mobile cutaneous outgrowths. The very large ears are fused in front at the base. A very typical feature of this family is the T-shape of the last joint of the tail which supports the hind edge of the interfemoral patagium.

Far from its African relations, the Javanese Slit-faced bat *(Nycteris javanica)* is found in Southeast Asia.

False Vampires (Megadermatidae)

The species of this family are closely related to the Slit-faced bats. Many systematists still combine them into a single family. The family of Old World False Vampires contains only a few species. They are distinguished by a large, conspicuous leaf-like expansion of skin around the nostrils which can take many forms. It lends the bat a very bizarre appearance. For example, the curled edges of the nose leaf of the African Yellow-winged bat *(Lavia frons)* give it the shape of a three-pronged harpoon blade. That of another species is lyre-shaped and has earned it its name of *Megaderma lyra*. The ears of these bats are large and the tragus is bifid. In spite of the absence of caudal vertebrae, the interfemoral patagium is well developed.

The Australian False Vampire bat *(Macroderma gigas)* is among the largest of the Microchiroptera. Although these bats are not blood feeders, but live on a diet of insects and small vertebrates, their grotesque appearance has made them the prototype of the vampire in illustrations and in horror films. For this reason, the family was given the vernacular name of False Vampires.

And what is so fearful about these bats? Undoubtedly the total impression they produce. The light-coloured creatures with a face almost pure white, achieve a wing span of more than 70 cm. A massive skull with large eyes, a huge nose leaf and great ears which also show only very slight pigmentation all intensify the extraordinary impression.

Since the False Vampire bats are solitary, it is not easy to discover them when they have withdrawn into their retreats during the day. So far, little is known about the habits of this exciting species.

Horseshoe bats (Rhinolophidae) and Old World Leaf-nosed bats (Hipposideridae)

These two Old World families are so closely linked that in the literature they are quite frequently dealt with as one. Both possess curious fleshy appendages surrounding the nostrils, from which the vernacular names are derived.

In the Rhinolophids, a "horseshoe-shaped" flap of skin covers the upper lip and surrounds the nostrils. Further membranous structures over the nose include a narrow, lengthwise ridge and an upright, pointed blade, the lancet. In each species, these features are species-characteristic and provide a reliable guide to the systematist. We shall consider later their function in focussing the beams of sound during the emission of ultrasonic pulses. The ears of Horseshoe bats are relatively large. They lack the tragus present in the members of other families of bats.

There are about 70 species, most of which are cave dwellers. They live communally, but when roosting, are careful to ensure that a certain distance separates each bat from its neighbour. The normal position at rest is a typical one in which the delicate wing membranes are folded round the body like a cloak. Found in their winter roost, the Horseshoe bats resemble dried fruits hanging freely suspended from the roof of the cave. In most species, including the European, the colour of the fur is an inconspicuous dark grey or dark brown. But some are of a striking orange-red. The hairs are long and fine, producing a soft, furry impression. All Horseshoe bats are insectivorous. Those which live in the temperate zone, hibernate during cold winter weather.

North of the Alps, as far as the Hercynean mountains and in the south of England, only two species can be found, and unfortunately their numbers are declining all the time; they are the Greater and Lesser Horseshoe bats (*Rhinolophus ferrumequinum* and *Rhinolophus hipposideros*). Whereas in the former, the length of head and body together reaches 7 cm, in the latter it is no more than 4 cm, making it the dwarf in this family.

The Hipposiderids, which are closely related to the Rhinolophids, consist of about 60 species. They inhabit tropical and subtropical Africa, Asia Minor, India and Southeast Asia as far as Australia. No species has extended its range northwards as far as Europe. In most of the members of the family, a nose leaf of rather simpler construction surrounds the nostrils. In some species, these skin flaps are grouped like the petals of a flower round the nostrils (*Anthops ornatus*). A structure corresponding to the lancet of the Rhinolophids, only this time shallow oval in form, is also found in *Hipposideros commersoni*. Or it can be subdivided into several leaflets, as in the Trefoil Leaf-nosed bat (*Triaenops persicus*) or the Trident Leaf-nosed bat (*Asellia tridens*).

Most members of this family are insectivorous, but some large species are also carnivorous. During the day, they roost in buildings or caves, either alone or in colonies which may consist of more than a thousand bats. In comparison with other families, the range of colouring among the Hipposiderids is strikingly wide with bright orange shades predominating. In the small South African Lesser Leaf-nosed bat (*Hipposideros caffer*) that is widespread in Africa, there are two colour variants, one being a dark grey-brown and one a glowing reddish-brown. Similar examples of dimorphism have also been described among certain Rhinolophids. The large species Commerson's Leaf-nosed bat (*Hipposideros commersoni*) of Africa reaches a head and body length of 11 cm, making it one of the larger forms among the Microchiroptera.

Spear-nosed bats (Phyllostomidae)

The New World family of Spear-nosed bats provides interesting parallels to the families of the Old World, which contain those species with the most complex and highly elaborated nasal attachments. As the name implies, members of this family also possess a nose leaf.

There are some 140 species in this family, and they live mainly in the tropical regions of Central and South America. In addition to the nose leaf, there are other features which provide evidence of evolutionary developments parallel with those found in the distant families of the Old World. Certain species without nose leaves have developed fleshy foliaceous outgrowths in the form of chin leaves. In others, the snout region is greatly extended, an indication, as in the case of the Long-tongued Fruit bats, that these species are nectar feeders. On the basis of these varied and sometimes extreme developments within the single family, the Spear-nosed bats are divided into several major subfamilies. Some systematists consider that certain of them represent distinct families. The family group of Spear-nosed bats includes both small forms with a head and body length of 4.5 cm, as well as some that are 15 cm long. Apart from body size, other features are extremely diverse. There are great differences in ear size; in some species the interfemoral membrane is fully developed, while in others it is reduced or completely absent. In the latter case, the caudal vertebrae are correspondingly regressed.

Among the typical Spear-nosed bats in the narrowest sense (Phyllostominae) there are species with very singular cuticular structures. These in many cases have earned the creatures names which are a reference to the shape of the nasal appendage. For example, the nose leaf of the Sword-nosed bat *(Lonchorhina aurita)* is in the shape of a spearhead and reaches the considerable length of 2 cm, while the small nose leaf of the Spear-nosed bat *(Phyllostomus hastatus)* is much like the tip of a lance. The Spear-nosed bats are large creatures with a wing span of up to 55 cm. They live on insects and fruit, but are also prepared to take small vertebrates. With their large canine teeth they are able to seize small birds and bats—in captivity, even mice—kill them by crushing and devour them. Observations of these bats in captivity have shown that they always eat the prey head first, supporting it skilfully by the claw of the thumb.

The Spear-nosed bats roost during the day in underground chambers and caves as well as in buildings, churches and hollow trees. They are sometimes found in thousands.

This subfamily contains the largest species of "insectivorous" bat in the New World, the Giant Spear-nosed bat *(Vampyrum spectrum)*. It achieves a wing span of 70 to 90 cm. The large ears and dagger-like nasal appendage give the bat a grotesque appearance. It is not surprising that this species also accords well with the popular conception of a vampire, and for this reason was believed by early writers to feed on blood. Although it has long been recognized that this is not so, the name "False Vampire" has continued to be used in many places. Even the scientific name reflects this error.

The predominantly fruit-eating Flying Foxes of the Old World have their counterpart in the fruit-eating species of certain subfamilies of Spear-nosed bats. It is interesting to observe how this parallel development in feeding habits has led to the same morphological changes. The fruit eaters of the eastern hemisphere as of the western show considerable broadening and flattening of the molars.

Of the Short-tailed Spear-nosed bats (Carolliinae), the Seba's Short-tailed bat *(Carollia perspicillata)* is the most widespread. It inhabits an area extending from Mexico to Southern Brazil. These bats live mainly on wild figs, bananas and guavas. The subfamily of fruit-eating Spear-nosed bats with the largest number of species is the Stenoderminae. These medium-sized bats are stoutly built and in most genera are distinguished by a small nose leaf with a spear, with an additional horseshoe-shaped membranous structure at the base. In some cases, the dark brownish-grey fur typical of these species is marked with four light-coloured longitudinal stripes on the head (*Artibeus* spp.). In addition, some species, such as *Uroderma bilobatum* have a light stripe along the middle of the back.

All but a few species of Stenoderminae spend the day in small groups, roosting among the foliage of trees. Many observers believe that some small *Artibeus* species and *Uroderma* are able to form the leaves of palm trees into a tent-like roof which protects them from sun, rain and natural enemies. This feature has earned them the name of Tent-building bats or Tent bats.

Like Old World fruit bats, the "fruit vampires" also prefer to eat soft juicy fruits from which they frequently extract only the juice. The remains are allowed to drop to the ground where they accumulate in large quantities beneath feeding trees or regular resting sites.

The extremes which facial conformation can achieve in bats is shown among the Stenodermids by the Wrinkle-faced bat *(Centurio senex)*. This species, which occurs primarily in Central America, has no nose leaf, but the skin of the face which is hairless, is arranged in an intricate pattern of wrinkles, folds and fleshy lobes producing a grotesque appearance of senility.

A curious modification in the attachment of the wing membranes can be seen in the Naked-backed bats belonging to the subfamily of Leaf-chinned bats (Chilonycterinae). The name Naked-backed bat is, in fact, misleading, for the bat's back is furred quite normally. Since, however, both in the Greater *(Pteronotus suapurensis)* and in the Lesser Naked-backed bat *(Pteronotus davyi)* the wing membranes are attached at the centre line of the back, the impression is given that the back is bare. These bats roost during the day in caves, in colonies of various sizes. The Frankfurt zoologist Felten reports that they prefer day-time quarters with very high relative humidity and a temperature of 38°C. In this suffocatingly hot and humid atmosphere, where the nauseous vapours emanating from vast quantities of droppings make it impossible for humans to breathe, the creatures obviously feel perfectly at home, and even bring up their young here.

One of the small number of Spear-nosed bats found in the southern states of the U.S.A. is the Leaf-chinned bat *Mormoops megalophylla*. This reddish-brown, medium-sized species has been reported in Arizona and Texas. Colonies of up to 4000 bats spend summer and winter in caves, mine galleries and tunnels. Like Horseshoe bats, they do not cluster closely together, but carefully avoid direct bodily contact with their neighbour. The skull of this insectivorous species is extremely compressed. The neurocranium curves upwards in a dome almost at right angles to the facial cranium, in a manner reminiscent of the skull shape of the pug breed of dog.

Another inhabitant of Arizona is the Californian Spear-nosed bat *(Macrotus waterhousei)*. It has very large ears and can easily be distinguished from other species of similar appearance by the presence of a triangular nose leaf. This species is also insectivorous and roosts underground during the day.

Among those species of Phyllostomids in the subfamily of Nectar-feeding Spear-nosed bats (Glossophaginae), three representatives are found in the southern states of North America. These are the Mexican Long-tongued bat *(Choeronycteris mexicana)*, the Nectar bat *Leptonycteris nivalis* and Sanborn's Nectar bat *(Leptonycteris sanborni)*. All species possess an elongate skull and a small nose leaf at the end of the snout. The tongue is long and highly extensible with a concentration of bristle-like papillae at the tip. These features show that the bats are extremely well adapted to obtaining food from flowers.

The Long-nosed bats roost communally during the day in caves and mine galleries. At night, they seek their food from the flowers of agaves, yucca trees and various cactus plants. They will also eat insects. Since these species do not hibernate, they leave their habitats in the cold season and migrate south from the United States into neighbouring Mexico.

Of the remaining New World families of bats, only a few species are known and little research has been carried out into their way of life. True Vampire bats (Desmodontidae) will be considered in a separate chapter.

Fisherman bats (Noctilionidae)

These bats have no nose leaf, but a fleshy upper lip, which is divided by a vertical fold. This feature has given the bats the vernacular name of "hare-lipped bats". The family is particularly noteworthy, since one of its two species *(Noctilio leporinus)* is specialized as a fish eater. It also eats insects, as does the smaller species in this family, *Noctilio labialis*. As an adaptation to the fishing habit, the hind feet of the Fish-eating or Fisherman bats are much enlarged and are furnished with strong curved claws. The brilliant rufous colouring of the males distinguishes them from the greyish-brown of the females. These species are distributed across a wide range from Mexico to Argentina.

Funnel-eared bats (Natalidae)

Bats of this small family inhabit tropical Central and South America. Forms so far found have no nose leaf. They have a long tail and particularly long hind legs. Indeed, the length of the hind legs can exceed that of the head and body together. The large, funnel-shaped ears have earned the name of Funnel-eared bats for members of the genus *Natalus*. They are insect feeders and roost during the day in caves.

Thumbless or Smoky bats (Furipteridae)

This family is closely related to the Funnel-eared bats. In the two species, the thumb is so rudimentary that only a tiny non-functioning vestigial claw is visible externally. Representatives of this family are among the smallest species of bats. Head and body measured together scarcely reach 5 cm. The most striking feature of these small bats is their large, funnel-shaped ears.

Among those families that are distributed throughout the world are the Sheath-tailed bats (Emballonuridae), the Free-tailed bats (Molossidae) and the Vespertilionid bats (Vespertilionidae). Their members, like those of certain families already mentioned, have no nose leaf, that is, they are "simple-nosed". One could almost regret the lack of such an ideal identification feature, particularly since these three families comprise more than half of all species of bats. It is not always simple to detect the minute differences which distinguish the many species one from another.

Sheath-tailed bats (Emballonuridae)

The members of this family, some 50 species, are small to medium sized bats that are found in the tropical and subtropical regions of the Old World, and also in large numbers in the warmer regions of America. Their name refers to the particular structure of the tail, part of which extends freely beyond the interfemoral membrane. In flight, many of the species are able to retract this part into a sheath of skin in the membrane. Some species have unusual markings on the fur, which provide a useful, protective camouflage when they are roosting during the day on the branches of forest trees. Marking is sometimes in the form of two light-coloured stripes running the length of the back as far as the tail membrane, as, for example, in the Greater White-lined bat (*Saccopteryx bilineata*). In the front part of the wing membrane between shoulder and elbow, this species has conspicuous wing sacs which produce a strong-smelling glandular secretion. They are more highly developed in the male and clearly have a sexual function. A very striking group within this family is the Ghost bats (*Diclidurus* spp.), that is entirely white. It is not clear whether this unusual colouring is of any biological advantage to the species.

The best-known and most widely distributed species of Emballonurids in Africa are the Tomb bats (*Taphozous* spp.). They are also found in Southern Asia, Australia and on various islands in the South Pacific. They are medium-sized bats weighing between 10 and 30 g. They were given the name of Tomb bats by scientists who accompanied Napoleon on his campaigns to Egypt and who first discovered them in the burial chambers of the Pyramids. But it has since been established that not all species roost in gloomy underground chambers. Many of them prefer open terrain and roost on tree trunks or under roofs.

Free-tailed bats (Molossidae)

This family contains some 90 species which are distributed throughout the warmer regions of the world. The Molossids are well adapted to various climatic conditions. In Africa, Kulzer found them in almost every climatic zone. In these bats, the end of the tail projects well beyond the edge of the interfemoral membrane; this feature has earned them their name. In flight, however, the interfemoral membrane can be slid down over the tail, producing an active enlargement of the bearing surface.

A striking feature of many Molossids is the broad, bulky head. The thick, angular ears lend the head a massive aspect, which in many species is given a grotesque quality by large numbers of folds and warts on the upper lip. The long, narrow wings indicate that these bats are excellent, long-distance flyers, but are not particularly manoeuvrable. On the ground, they can run with considerable agility on powerful legs, with wings tightly folded. The Molossids are insectivorous. They live communally, often in large colonies that can number up to a million individuals. With so many different species, it is not surprising to find them in a wide variety of habitats, in caves, on trees and in buildings. They have even been observed to roost under galvanized iron roofs where the temperatures at midday reach extraordinarily high levels. In Egypt, these species are often found in ancient burial chambers, in India they live in temples.

In some roosts that have been used continually for centuries, vast quantities of droppings have accumulated underneath the roosts as guano, which can be collected and marketed as a fertilizer. The most spectacular example of mass congregations of bats can be seen in the summer roosts of the Guano bats *(Tadarida brasiliensis)* in the Carlsbad Caverns in New Mexico, U.S.A. In the early sixties, the number of bats living here in quite a small space was estimated to be some four to five million. Among mammals, only bats have been found in vast concentrations of this kind. Unfortunately, their numbers have declined sharply in recent years. Later chapters will examine various aspects of life in vast colonies such as these.

Among Molossids, the large Naked bats (*Cheiromeles* spp.) are most bizarre in appearance. These species, which live in Southeast Asia, are almost completely hairless. Black, bristly hairs grow only on the large throat sack and the "collar" of loose folds of skin round the neck. The wings start at the mid point of the back, and folds of skin form a pouch along the sides of the body in which the wing membrane is stowed when the bat is resting.

Vespertilionid bats (Vespertilionidae)

This family comprises some 320 species, that is, a third of all known bats. Vespertilionids represent the largest part of the bat fauna of Europe and North America, both in number of species and number of individuals. 24 species of Vespertilionid bats live in Europe, while 30 species of this family are found in North America. It should be emphasized that some species are very common and widely distributed, whereas others are quite narrowly restricted in range and are considerable rarities among our fauna.

The wide variety of species within the family is reflected on the one hand in differences in body size and other morphological features; on the other hand, in a broad range of variations in habit and habitat. In addition to pigmy forms weighing no more than 3 g, there are quite large species which can weigh 80 g. With such an abundance of forms, it is difficult to specify features that are common to all members of this large family. As the British zoologists Yalden and Morris pertinently remark, "perhaps the best generalisation is that Vespertilionids are those bats which, externally at least, lack the special characters of other families".

In all species, the tail is well developed and usually integrated into the interfemoral membrane. Apart from a few exceptions in Australia, the bats have simple noses. The majority of them are insectivorous and are capable of nocturnal orientation by means of ultrasonic echolocation.

In a family so rich in species, it is impossible to attempt a comprehensive survey of all Vespertilionids. Certain European species have therefore been selected. In many cases, these bats or close relations of theirs, also inhabit other continents, where they exhibit numerous similarities in appearance and habit to their European cousins.

There are the Mouse-eared bats of the genus *Myotis*, which, as cave dwellers, spend at least the winter season in underground quarters. In summer, they are often found in buildings, where the Large Mouse-eared bat (*Myotis myotis*) (body size 8 cm, wing span up to 40 cm) shows a preference for the spacious roof vaults of old buildings, particularly churches. There are some 60 species of Mouse-eared bats; systematic differentiation is based particularly on the size and shape of ear, tragus and teeth. In the case of other groups of Vespertilionids, such as the Pipistrelle, Noctule, Barbastelle and Long-eared bat, the ear and teeth once again play an important part as distinguishing features in identifying species.

Of the 24 European species of Vespertilionid bats alone, ten belong to the genus of Mouse-eared bats, *Myotis*. Older accounts invariably state that the Large Mouse-eared bat is by far the most common species in Europe, where it is usually found in summer roosting in large colonies. Unfortunately, this can no longer be claimed today. The decline in the numbers of this admirable and beneficial species gives cause for concern.

The other *Myotis* species occurring in Europe, and closely related to the Large Mouse-eared bats, are medium-sized animals measuring 4 to 5 cm in length from snout to tail base, usually coloured greyish-brown on the back and lighter yellowish-grey or whitish-grey on

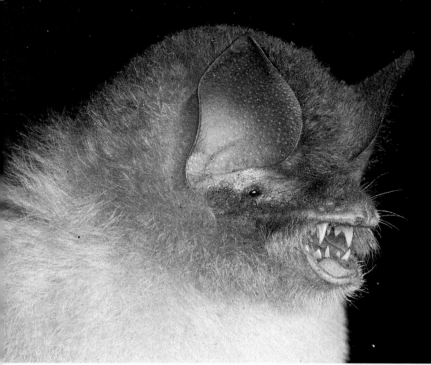

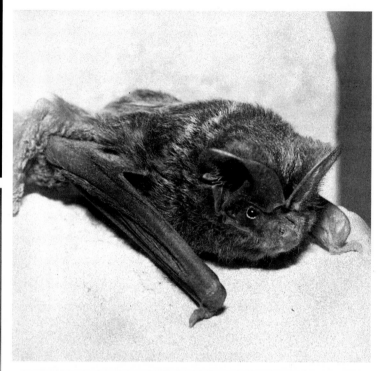

48 Barbastelle (*Barbastella barbastellus*; Vespertilionidae). This species is dark-brown to black in colour; the ears are joined together centrally at their bases. The Barbastelle is widely distributed in Europe but numbers are never large.

49 Large Mouse-eared bat (*Myotis myotis*; Vespertilionidae). The largest European representative of the Vespertilionid bats. Body weight up to 36 g; wing span 35 to 43 cm. Large Mouse-eared bats live communally, frequently in large colonies, but their numbers are declining.

46 *Natalus stramineus*. A small bat belonging to the family of Funnel-eared bats (Natalidae). Habitat: Central and South America.

47 Pipistrelle *(Pipistrellus pipistrellus)*. The smallest species of bat in Europe (body weight 3–8 g, wing span about 20 cm). This species, common in many places, lives communally and has considerable resistance to cold.

51   Northern bat (*Eptesicus nils-soni;* Vespertilionidae)

52   Geoffroy's bat (*Myotis emar-ginatus;* Vespertilionidae)

53   Brandt's bat (*Myotis brandti;* Vespertilionidae)

76

54 Natterer's bat (*Myotis nattereri;* Vespertilionidae) taking flight. In this medium-sized bat, the hind margin of the interfemoral membrane is furnished with numerous stiff hairs.

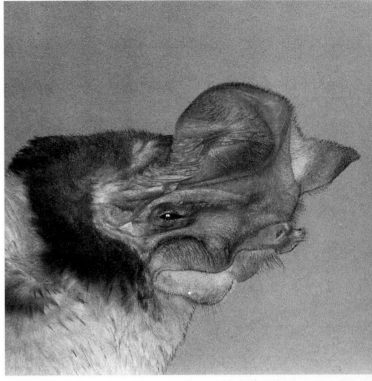

55 Brown Long-eared bat (*Plecotus auritus*; Vespertilionidae). The appearance of the head is dominated by the very long ears. The large number of ear pleats indicate that the ear can be furled and folded. During hibernation, the bats fold the ears down along the side of the body and tuck them under the wings. This species is frequently found in Europe. In summer, they often inhabit nesting boxes.

56 *Otomops martiensseni* (Molossidae). A Free-tailed bat from Africa. The remarkable structure of the snout region lends the bats an extremely odd appearance.

57 *Tadarida hindei* (Molossidae). A representative of the African Free-tailed bats.

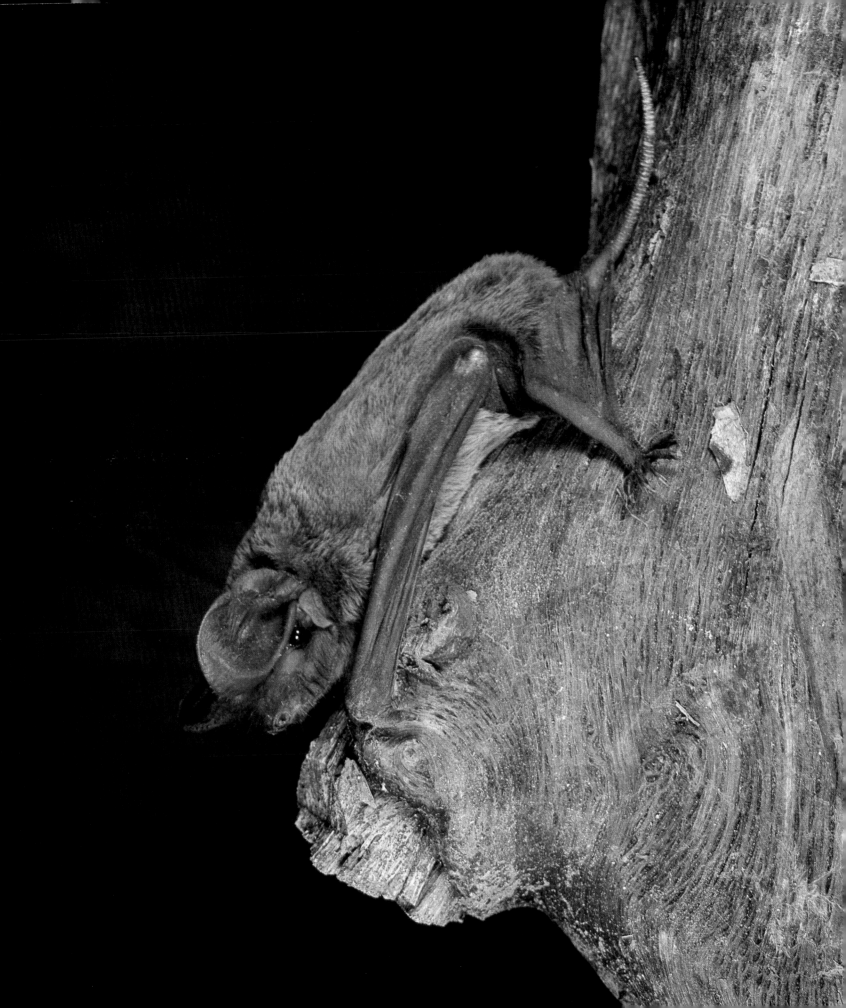

the underside. They include the rare Bechstein's bat (*Myotis bechsteini*) which spends the summer in hollow trees and the nesting boxes of birds. Natterer's bat (*Myotis nattereri*) is distinguished by a fringe of fine hairs on the back edge of the interfemoral patagium. It inhabits well-wooded regions. A rather rarer species is the Notch-eared bat or Geoffroy's bat (*Myotis emarginatus*), found principally in southern Europe. A more common species is the Daubenton's or Water bat (*Myotis daubentoni*), frequently found near water. In the summer, they roost during the day in crevices in the walls of old bridges, in buildings and in hollow trees. At night, they skim low over the surface of ponds and streams to catch insects. Other relations of the Mouse-eared bat include the Whiskered bats. It was established only in the last ten years that there are two species in Europe, the Whiskered bat (*Myotis mystacinus*) and the Brandt's bat (*Myotis brandti*). They are rare creatures and little is known of their habits and their distribution.

The smallest species are found among the Pipistrelles that are also distributed throughout the world, apart from South America. The European species can easily be distinguished from other indigenous species. But the four found here are extremely similar in appearance, and the exact identification of a Pipistrelle (*Pipistrellus pipistrellus*), Nathusius' Pipistrelle (*Pipistrellus nathusii*), Kuhl's Pipistrelle (*Pipistrellus kuhli*) and Savi's Pipistrelle (*Pipistrellus savii*) can cause difficulty even to the specialist. Whereas the European species set up their summer roosts in and on buildings, in hollow trees and nesting boxes, the Banana bats (*Pipistrellus nanus*) living in Africa, often roost in young banana leaves that have not yet unrolled.

Pipistrelles have proved to be more common and more widely distributed in Europe than had hitherto been realized. Because of their small size and their habit of concealing themselves in narrow crevices, they have to a great extent successfully eluded observation. Increasing numbers of new roosts have been reported in some rural areas, but in the U. K. monitored colonies have decreased markedly in recent years. The bats are obviously not excessively sensitive to cold and wet weather, and winter roosts with more than 1000 bats have been found, even in churches.

In the autumn, as they make their way to their winter sites, these small creatures can cause a good deal of disturbance. At this time, whole flocks of Pipistrelles sometimes invade some particular corner of a house which they have never entered previously. One can well imagine the reaction of the householders when, next morning, they discover these harmless creatures in, say, the folds of their bedroom curtains. After autumn intrusions of this kind, Pipistrelles have also been found inside vases, behind picture frames and door ledges, under floorboards and between double windows. An "attack" of this kind is no cause for panic. It is much more important to help the creatures to escape.

Many species of Vespertilionid bats find their ideal habitat on and in the dwellings of human beings, and for this reason are sometimes called house bats. Others seem never to roost in buildings; they live in trees and are designated "tree bats". A typical tree bat is the Common Noctule (*Nyctalus noctula*). It is one of the larger European species; the ears and roundish tragus are relatively small. Noctules often leave their roosts early, even before sunset, and it is sometimes possible to observe them in rapid flight high above the treetops. In contrast to the grey fur of the Mouse-eared bats, that of the Noctule is reddish-brown in colour. The short, dense fur has a silky sheen.

Another of the larger species is the Serotine or Broad-winged bat (*Eptesicus serotinus*). These bats enjoy the proximity of human settlements. They can often be observed on warm summer evenings flying low in search of insects near trees in town, in gardens and close to houses. Since the wings are much broader and less pointed than those of Noctules, flight is correspondingly slower and more leisurely. In their winter roosts, the Serotines rarely hang freely suspended from a roof but more often hide away in crevices in rocks. So it is very difficult to find them.

Closely related to the European species is the North American Big Brown bat *(Eptesicus fuscus)*. It too prefers buildings for its day-time roosting site. The genus *Eptesicus* comprises many very small Vespertilionids. In an African species of *Eptesicus*, the newly-born young are described as no larger than bees.

The European Northern bat *(Eptesicus nilssoni)* is characterized by a particularly high resistance to cold. The range of this species extends northwards as far as the Arctic Circle and it is found on mountains up to an altitude of 2000 m. The Red bat *(Lasiurus borealis)* and the larger Hoary bat *(Lasiurus cinereus)* are two American species that penetrate to the far north. In summer, these bats roost in trees and bushes where they suspend themselves from trunks and branches. Usually they are so well concealed among the foliage that they are protected both from inclement weather and from enemies. Since they often hang by one foot only, they can, at a cursory glance, easily be mistaken for a withered leaf. In these species, too, the "tree bats" in contrast to the "house bats" have richer and more varied colouring. In the male of the Red bat in particular, the orange-red colour is especially intense. Another striking feature is that in the *Lasiurus* species, the upper surface of the interfemoral membrane is completely or partially covered with dense fur. In autumn, these species cover long distances to the southern states of the U.S.A., where they spend the win-

ter. But they have considerable resistance to cold, and the Red bat has been observed flying and feeding in the evenings of warmer winter days.

A feature unusual in *Lasiurus* is the number of young that are born. In contrast to most bat species, in which the female gives birth to only one young, multiple births appear to be fairly common among the *Lasiurus* species. In the case of Red bats, a total of up to four young is not unusual, while twins occur frequently among Hoary bats and also the European Common Noctule *(Nyctalus noctula)*.

Because of their exceptional powers of flight, these bats have been able to cross from the American mainland to the Hawaiian Islands almost 4000 km away. It is inconceivable that they could cover this distance in continuous flight. It must have been possible for them to "pause for breath" by resting on the rigging of ships on the way. But the fact remains that *Lasiurus cinereus* has been living there for more than a century as the only species of bat, and in that time has already developed the specific features of an island race. It has also been recorded several times in Iceland and once in Orkney.

Among those Vespertilionids that are widespread in Europe, mention should also be made of the Barbastelle *(Barbastella barbastellus)* and the Long-eared bat *(Plecotus* spp.). These are medium-sized species weighing between 5 and 8 g. They roost in summer on or in buildings. The former may be found behind window shutters and wall panelling, while the latter prefer to roost behind beams and rafters in roof spaces. They are also found in hollow trees and nesting boxes.

Barbastelles are dark, almost black, in colour, while the tips of the hairs on the back gleam white, giving the bat a frosted appearance. The broad, stunted ears are joined at the base by a ridge of skin. The nose is flattened, so that the face is not unlike that of a small pug dog.

A distinctive feature of the Grey and Brown Long-eared bats *(Plecotus austriacus* and *P. auritus)* is the exceptional length of the ears, which sometimes are three times the length of the head. These sound-sensing devices are so large that they quite overshadow the small face. But during hibernation and in periods of day-time sleep, nothing is seen of these great "sonar receivers". At these times, only the narrow tragus is left pointing forwards, while the ears themselves are furled, folded backwards and concealed under the wings.

Among the Long-eared species that inhabit the south-west of the U.S.A., mention should be made of the Pallid bat *(Antrozous pallidus)*. In this species, the fur on the upper surface of the body is a pale yellowish colour with brownish-grey tips. The underside is also light-coloured. The loss of dark pigmentation from the creature's coat has been associated with the nature of its habitat. It prefers to live in dry areas of steppe, where in summer, it roosts during the day in caves, ruins and buildings. It feeds largely on insects which it catches as it flies close to the ground, or it may also take them from the ground or from leaves. Remnants of food found in the roosts show that these bats also eat scorpions and small reptiles.

Where bats live

The life of bats, with its phases of rest and activity, is strictly adapted to the alternating rhythm of night and day. Like all mammals, bats have two territorial regions, one of which offers protection during periods of reduced activity when the bats are able to rest and satisfy social needs, and the other through which they move in search of food.

The day roost is just as important an element in the life of bats as is the hunting territory. Only if there is a day roost available to them, is it possible for bats to colonize a particular region. It is not the availability of food alone which affects the distribution of bats and their numbers in a particular region, but also the existence of suitable roosting quarters.

These are especially vital in the case of bats since these animals are unable to prepare refuges for themselves in the form of burrows, hollows or nests.

The simplest solution to the accommodation problem, although perhaps not the most ideal, is that adopted by the large fruit bats. During the day, they roost on the branches of large trees. We have already seen how they brave all weathers and how skilfully they manage to achieve a measure of protection. Most of the smaller forms of bats are not able to spend the day hanging from a branch. Sun, wind, rain, fluctuations in temperature and not least the attention of enemies would affect them and their young so adversely that the survival of the species would be endangered. A roosting site which provides more protection is essential.

Since they cannot construct one themselves, they must depend on finding and using shelters that already exist. Bats have settled in some quite surprising sites, and their roosts show a wide variety of forms. In addition to those offered by the natural environment, they also choose the homes of other animals as well as buildings inhabited by man. The fact that bats make use of existing caves and hollows in trees in which to live, or that they inhabit the underground burrows, nesting hollows or nests of other animals is usually termed ecological parasitism. For lack of natural retreats, bats in many areas have settled in or on buildings erected by man, where they have found refuges with a microclimate in keeping with their biological requirements. In addition, mine workings, quarries, bridges and tunnels, even the hollow concrete columns of street lights have all been considered as a welcome extension of the range of available accommodation and have been colonized accordingly.

Tree-dwelling bats

Today, many bats, like their ancestors, are arboreal. Most of the species found on or in trees, live in the tropics. The variety of potential dwellings which a tree can offer is surprisingly wide, and bats have discovered and exploited virtually every possibility for colonization. As many as twenty different dwelling sites on sound and decaying trees have been listed.

The roots alone are greatly in demand as a living area. The Indian Short-nosed Fruit bat (Cynopterus sphinx), for example, has been found living among the aerial roots of fig trees. In the evening, it climbs first up the roots and then up the trunk to a branch, before setting off on its nocturnal flight. In Africa, species of Epauletted Fruit bats (Epomophorus anurus) and of Old World Leaf-nosed bats (Hipposideros beatus) have been found among tree roots projecting from the sloping sides of river banks.

In the next stage of the tree, the region of the trunk, a few species are found which roost in the open, pressed up against the tree bark. This primitive form of roost is found in particular among representatives of the Sheath-tailed bats such as the African Tomb bat *(Taphozous mauritianus)* or the South American Greater White-lined bat *(Saccopteryx bilineata)*. Since it affords scarcely any protection, the bats get little rest during the day. As soon as danger approaches, they scuttle rapidly to the other side of the trunk or fly to a different tree. In Southeast Asia, two small species of Vespertilionid bats with flattened skulls *(Tylonycteris* spp.) have elected to roost in the hollows in bamboo stems excavated by insect larvae. They creep into the bamboo canes through narrow vertical slits made by beetles. Hollows of this kind have been found to contain individual bats, usually males, but occasionally, small colonies of ten to twelve animals of both sexes.

Large species of African Epauletted Fruit bats roost in the tangled branches and thick foliage of old trees. They prefer branches that extend far out across rivers or lakes. From here, they can easily take flight without becoming entangled in the dense thickets of the forest. On the other hand, the dark roof of leaves provides adequate protection from sun and rain. In contrast, the degree of protection afforded by the tree is insignificant in the case of the Asiatic species of *Pteropus*. Over the years, their traditional roosting trees have been stripped of bark and foliage by thousands of claws so that the bats hang in full view on the dry branches.

Although the tree roosts are often close to human habitations, the bats quickly learned that no danger threatens them from that quarter. The religion of the country forbids its adherents to kill bats. As a result, it has been possible for many colonies of fruit bats to become established in such populous cities as Bombay. The constant stream of people thronging the streets of the town seems only to enhance the bats' sense of security. Only an attempt to climb the tree will cause the entire colony to take flight.

Previously, large numbers of fruit bats in Australia also established themselves close to human settlements "for reasons of safety". But they were forced to move away, for here neither religion nor law protected them. They were increasingly persecuted and their numbers drastically reduced; they had no alternative but to withdraw into sparsely populated areas.

The small species of fruit bats and various members of the American Spear-nosed bats, which are also arboreal, are very difficult to discern when roosting. They hang quietly among dense foliage and many species gain additional protection from the striped markings on their fur, as the outline of the body is completely obliterated in the play of light and shade. The *Lasiurus* species which in summer roost in the deciduous forests of North America are forced to leave their summer quarters in autumn when the leaves begin to fall. Those species which live all the year round in the southern states are reported to move at this time from apricot trees on to evergreen orange trees.

Among cultivated trees, palm and banana trees offer particularly favourable living conditions to bats, and are regularly colonized by a large number of species. In addition to Short-nosed Fruit bats *(Cynopterus sphinx)*, representatives of other bat families are also found in the crowns of palm trees in India. In Cuba and other Central American countries, large colonies of Free-tailed bats *(Tadarida laticaudata yucatanica* and *Tadarida minuta)* live in the withered foliage of tall palms. One species of tree is such a typical domicile for bats that botanists gave it the scientific name of *Copernicia vespertilionum*, the Bat Palm. Those trees that house bats are easily recognized by a thick layer of droppings on the ground round the trunk. Since the lower part of the tufty foliage of these trees is a thick curtain of dried-out fronds, it offers excellent protection to its tenants. The number of bats on

Possible roosts for bats on and in trees (after Greenhall, 1968)

one tree has been estimated at between two and three thousand.

On banana trees, several species of bats may be found together beneath the central ribs of the large hanging leaves. Even in regions where these trees have been introduced commercially, bats have not been slow to recognize that the large leaves offer an ideal protection from sun and rain. In Africa and South America, small species of fruit-eating bats live in banana trees. Pipistrelles often roost on clusters of banana fruits. In Africa, small species of Mouse-eared bats and Pipistrelles and in America, Sucker-footed bats (*Thyroptera* spp.) have been found inside young leaves that are still rolled up into a cone. The latter sit in small groups among the leaves, and in contrast to the habitual position of bats, roost with the

head upwards. The French zoologist Brosset reported finding Vespertilionid bats in that part of the tree where buds were forming on all banana plantations in Gabon. So specialized are the bats in seeking out this particular resting place that they follow in the wake of the sequence of planting. Each of the selected leaves thus provides accommodation for only twenty-four hours. After that time, it has unrolled so far that the bats are obliged to seek out a new banana leaf, still tightly rolled, for the following day.

Dead trees that have remained standing for decades, particularly in primeval forests, also offer ideal roosting sites. Many tropical species of forest-dwelling Rhinolophids (Horseshoe bats), Hipposiderids (Old World Leaf-nosed bats) and Molossids (Free-tailed bats) live in natural depressions and holes made by birds, and in spaces behind loose bark. In Africa, the Great Slit-faced bat

(*Nycteris grandis*) and the Old World Leaf-nosed bat *Hipposideros cyclops* rely on hollows in trees. In South America, the Giant Spear-nosed bat *(Vampyrum spectrum)* and the Common Vampire bat *(Desmodus rotundus)* are often found in hollow trees.

Certain European species are also found behind loose bark, in nesting holes made by woodpeckers and in knot-holes in branches. A typical arboreal bat is the Common Noctule *(Nyctalus noctula)* which is found in deciduous and coniferous forests. Hollow spaces inside trees situated close to river banks are favoured by the Daubenton's or Water bat *(Myotis daubentoni)*, while Long-eared bats *(Plecotus* spp.) can very often be found in hollows in fruit trees and in nesting boxes. If the bats make use of these roosts for a number of years, marks made by urine stains at the entry hole often betray their presence. It appears that decomposition of wood inside the tree brought about by the action of urine and faecal matter causes an increase in heat and humidity which is difficient to enable the Noctules to remain all winter in these quarters.

Inhabitants of natural and man-made caves

In addition to the large group of bats that live in trees and bushes, or even in grass and moss, there are probably just as many that have chosen to roost in natural or artificial habitats underground. In both tropical and temperate latitudes, many species in various families are found that at least occasionally are cave dwellers.

Whereas in Europe most species spend at least the cold season in underground habitats, in the tropic and subtropical regions of the world, underground chambers are the homes of bats throughout the year. Here they roost, here social activities are performed and the young are

born and tended. Almost every continent has certain caves that have become legendary as the roosts of hundreds of thousands, even millions of bats. These places are in the nature of family property, going back to ancient times.

On the island of Borneo there is the Niah Cave (Sarawak), where some 300,000 bats have been found to live. In the "Cave of Thieves" near Bombay (India), there are about 100,000 Serotines *(Eptesicus serotinus)*; no less than 500,000 Old World Leaf-nosed bats of the species *Hipposideros caffer* roost in the Falcon Cave of Belinga (Gabon). Unimaginably large numbers make up the vast colonies of Guano bats *(Tadarida brasiliensis)* in certain caves in Mexico and the southern states of the U.S.A. It has been estimated that in some caves, the annual total of bats has reached ten to twenty million. It will be shown later how numbers have declined alarmingly in the last twenty years. As darkness falls and these vast numbers of bats set out on their nocturnal flight, pouring forth in thousands from the cave entrances, it looks to the distant observer like the column of smoke from a volcano rising skywards. This unique natural phenomenon is used as a tourist attraction by the authorities in charge of the Carlsbad Caverns in New Mexico, U.S.A. Every evening during the summer months, hundreds of sightseers wait to watch as some half a million bats take flight. The exact time of the spectacle cannot be predicted. It depends upon the arrival of dusk, and between May and October, has been recorded to take place between 4.30 in the afternoon and 8 o'clock in the evening. When the young bats born in June become independent, they join in the evening flight. So, from mid July, there is a spectacular increase in the number of animals issuing from the caves.

Before the sensational event begins for the tourists at the Carlsbad Caverns, growing excitement among the bats inside the caves signals the impending departure. Awakened by their "internal clock", the creatures yawn and stretch, rousing any of their neighbours that may still be dozing. This is unavoidable, since up to 3000 bats may roost in a square metre of roof area. The first bats take wing and stimulate others. More and more of them make for the cave entrance where, at first, they circle irresolutely, until some unknown signal indicates the start of the flight. The exodus from the Carlsbad Caverns does not always take the same form. Sometimes the bats emerge like clouds of smoke; that is, for 1 to 2 minutes, a great swarm flies out, and then there is an interval, frequently no more than a few seconds, before the next swarm appears. This continues for some minutes, but finally, so many bats press forward that the emerging stream becomes unbroken. They have also been observed to emerge straight away as a continuous swarm that streams out steadily for some 10 to 15 minutes and ends just as abruptly. No one knows why. After 30 or 40 minutes it begins again, and then the rest of the bats come flying out.

Generally the bats leave their day-time roost in continuous flight. Some 5000 per minute emerge from the vast cave entrance, and at the end of an hour, the cave is empty, the spectacle is concluded. At first the bats spiral upwards to a height of 50 to 60 m above the cave entrance and then fly off in the direction of their principal feeding grounds. These are wooded hillsides which provide insects in great numbers. Yet if such masses of hungry animals are to be satisfied, the individual may have to remain on the wing for eight to ten hours to obtain all the food it needs. Within this period of one night, these small mammals, weighing 15 g and with a wing span of 25 cm, cover a distance of 70 km or more. It is unusual for a bat to return in less than three or four hours. The majority do not get back to the cave until dawn is breaking.

The return flight to the roosts, and to the young bats waiting there, takes on a different form. Some eye-witnesses have claimed that it is an even more impressive sight. The bats come in from a great height, and streaming downwards in headlong flight, they draw in their wings and disappear into the Stygian gloom of the labyrinth of caves. Because of the high speed of flight, the air begins to vibrate as it streams past the wings, and when simultaneously hundreds of bats skim towards the cave mouth, curious, eerie sounds are produced. Just as suddenly as the exit began, the return flight of the bats suddenly comes to an end; an impressive natural phenomenon which still holds many mysteries, and which has been taking place day after day each summer for many thousands of years.

Vast colonies on this scale are, of course, exceptional. Depending upon the size of caves, and—a critical consideration—on the conditions of temperature, humidity and light existing within them, the number and composition of the species found in different regions of the world varies greatly. Even today we are not able to explain which factors cause bats to consider one roosting site particularly suitable and to colonize it in thousands, and yet to avoid another, which as far as we can see is entirely similar. These interesting questions are still waiting to be answered. It is especially important to bats that there should be no draughts, since they cannot tolerate draughty conditions. Therefore they select enclosed systems of caves as their summer roosts. If the cave has a blind end, warm air can accumulate there and the temperature does not fall to below the critical level of 15°C. Summer roosts of the Greater Horseshoe bat (*Rhinolophus ferrumequinum*) and of the Long-winged bat (*Miniopterus schreibersi*) have, however, been found in which the average ambient temperature was only 10 to 13°C.

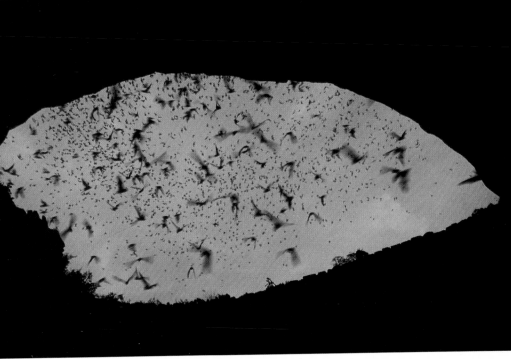

60　Swarms of Guano bats fly
across the evening sky on the way
to their feeding grounds.

61　Thousands of Guano bats
(*Tadarida brasiliensis*) set out in
the evening from their day-time
roost in the Carlsbad Caverns in
Texas, U.S.A.

62　Kalongs (*Pteropus vampyrus*)
leaving their tree roost

71 A Lesser Horseshoe bat
(Rhinolophus hipposideros) hibernating. The bat has enfolded itself
completely within its wing
membranes.

72 Three Natterer's bats *(Myotis
nattereri)* in hibernation

73 A group of Grey Mouse-
eared bats *(Myotis grisescens)* in
their winter roost.

74 A group of Large Mouse-
eared bats *(Myotis myotis)* in their
winter roost

75 Serotine *(Eptesicus serotinus).* This bat, in a state of lethargy,
has fallen from the wall of the
roost, and at first is completely
helpless. As a reflex action, it extends its wings and moves its extremities about in search of a support.

It is astonishing how well bats are able to tolerate the high concentrations of ammonia liberated from piles of droppings, and are still able to breathe in such an atmosphere. Experiments have shown that the strong smell of ammonia keeps enemies at bay, so that in effect it provides protection.

Just as in the European winter roosts, the individual species show distinct preferences for particular roosting places, so too within the caves of the tropics, there is a quite specific distribution of the species which is largely determined by conditions of light. Egyptian Fruit bats *(Rousettus aegyptiacus)* and members of the Sheath-tailed bats (Emballonurids) usually roost in the semi-darkness of the outer chambers. In the innermost recesses of the caves where no light penetrates, representatives of the Old World Leaf-nosed bats, Leaf-chinned bats and true Vampire bats can be found.

Bats have even succeeded in colonizing the desert sands of the Sahara, where they live in the subterranean channels of the irrigation systems. These are completely dark and pleasantly warm. Horseshoe bats and Vespertilionid bats are found there.

The great depth beneath the ground at which bats can be found is illustrated in reports from the U.S.A. Here, the galleries of a zinc mine north of New York serve as winter quarters to about 1000 Little Brown bats *(Myotis lucifugus)*. The majority of the bats roost in the upper passages at a depth of 200 m and with an ambient temperature of about 5 °C. But the deeper galleries are also visited, and contrary to all expectations, a bat has even been observed in the deepest gallery at a depth of 1160 m. Such depths are, of course, out of the question as winter roosts, since the prevailing temperature here is at least 25 °C.

Many of the species that live underground avoid spacious and high-roofed cave systems. They prefer narrow

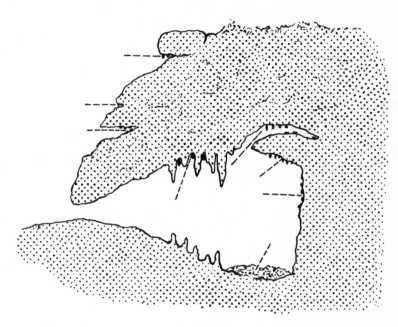

Roosts of bats in caves, tunnels and cellars (after Greenhall, 1968)

crevices in rocks and interstices between stones for their living quarters. In these cases, the bats are usually solitary or live in small groups. They conceal themselves very effectively and are difficult to observe.

In Egypt, Mouse-eared bats are found in the gravel of river beds, and on the Pacific coast of Mexico, the fish-eating bat *Pizonyx vivesi*, which is a Vespertilionid bat, has been found among loose stones and fragments of rock, where it often lives in company with the storm petrels that breed there. Rock crevices are a popular abode for various Free-tailed bats and Sheath-tailed bats. Any attempt to extract them from their roosts is unlikely to succeed since the slightest disturbance causes them to withdraw into the innermost recesses.

Inhabitants of buildings

Bats frequently find a modified form of the natural roosts that are available to them in and on buildings constructed by man. So it is not surprising that a wide range of species has adapted rapidly and taken over congenial houses, churches, temples, pyramids, towers and fortresses, occupying them "from cellar to attic". This explains why, in many regions, bat numbers are greater in towns and villages than in woodland and field. Quite often, the residents of a house do not realize that bats are sharing the same roof, unless the colonies assume such proportions that they become an annoyance to the occupants. Bats are frequently found in churches and places of worship, undoubtedly because here they are free from harassment. The lofty roof spaces of churches and castles are rarely disturbed, so that in addition to bats, other animals such as the barn owl (*Tyto alba*) will often roost and bear their young there. In Europe, Large Mouse-eared bats (*Myotis myotis*), Serotines (*Eptesicus serotinus*) and Long-eared bats (*Plecotus* spp.) are found during the summer in the roof spaces and belfries of churches and castles. In the winter, Common Noctules (*Nyctalus noctula*) and Pipistrelles (*Pipistrellus pipistrellus*) may be discovered in concealed hiding places in churches. The Church of Our Lady in Dresden housed one such winter roost until it was destroyed in February 1945. For decades, bats had lived here, high above the town without their presence being suspected. Not until 1926, when repairs were being carried out on the cupola, did workmen discover a large number of Noctules in a small space above the antependium of the altar. They hung up against the sandstone walls in rows one above the other like tiles on a roof. Their numbers were assessed at 800 to 1000 bats, grouped into several clusters. From that time on, counts carried out annually showed that every win-

Possible roosts for bats on and in buildings (after Greenhall, 1968)

ter, large numbers of males and females assembled in the warmest parts of the small attic room. The temperature there suited the requirements of the Noctules perfectly, so that virtually no losses were reported, except in the hardest of winters, when numbers could be reduced by half.

Other highly esteemed roosting sites are the ruins of ancient cult burial places, fortresses and defensive structures. In the Orient, Tomb bats (*Taphozous nudiventris*) are found in thousands in the ruins of former mausoleums. The Horseshoe bats of Europe, Asia and Africa like to live in the brickwork of old castles. Depending upon their geographical distribution, they roost in the company of Tomb bats, Mouse-tailed bats or Fruit bats like *Rousettus* or *Dobsonia*. In America, Sac-winged bats (*Saccopteryx*) have colonized the arcades of ancient Mayan temples. Like their relations in the Old World, such as various of the Tomb bats, they attach themselves to the outer walls of houses with no protection whatsoever. When the heat of the sun becomes excessive, they move to a cooler wall of the house.

Houses with cellars are, on the whole, restricted to the temperate and cool regions of the world. So it is only here that bats have the opportunity to occupy cellars; and they do so willingly when conditions are favourable. In Europe, bats frequently use cellars as an overwintering site. They roost in quiet, damp corners or dark wall crevices.

It is rare for humans and bats to share the same living quarters. Usually the bats are driven out or even killed by man. There are exceptions. In certain Indian villages, families of Hindus, to whom all animals are sacred and therefore protected, live in the same room as bats. The small bat lodgers roost on the smoke-blackened walls, knowing that no one will harm them. If anyone gets too close, they do not fly away but start to bite!

In many countries, these so-called "house bats" inhabit not only roof spaces and the joints and crevices of roof beams, but also window shutters, fascias, wainscoting, the frames of blinds and many other structural embellishments. Tiny Pipistrelles even lodge in joints between roof tiles and in thatched roofs. Such roosting places are met with equally in Europe, Algeria and India. In tropical America, small Free-tailed bats *(Molossus)* are to be found creeping out from under the roofs and out of cracks in walls as darkness falls and they prepare to set out on their nocturnal flights.

Bats that live in the nests and burrows of other animals

Ecological parasitism among the Chiroptera is also shown in their habit of taking over or sharing the living quarters and nests of other animals. For example, in England, Whiskered bats *(Myotis mystacinus)* have been observed in the nesting holes of sand martins.

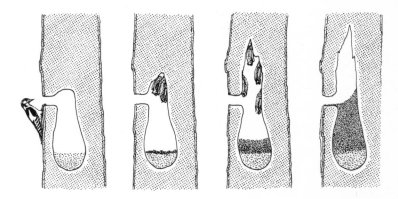

The development of a woodpecker's nesting hole into a bat roost (after Stratmann, 1978).

In various countries, colonies of bats have even been found in the sets, burrows and underground nests of the fox, badger, rabbit and porcupine. These holes in the ground are not always the most favourable of residences, particularly when the "owner" himself shares the occupancy. But if the environment offers nothing better, bats are prepared to live even there.

In Africa, Vespertilionids of the genus *Kerivoula* are often found roosting in the abandoned nests of birds, particularly weaver birds, and the American Mouse-eared bat *(Myotis velifer)* has been observed in the nesting holes of swallows under bridges. Even the nests of termites do not escape the attention of bats. In Trinidad and other places certain Spear-nosed bats *(Tonatia minuta)* have been known to establish themselves there, sharing these quarters with a small species of parrot.

Even more curious is the report of bats in spider's nests. Although there can be room there for only very few animals, it would seem from observations made in Gabon by the French zoologist Brosset that the Vespertilionid bat *Kerivoula harrisoni* regularly roosts under the webs of the *Agalena* spider. In doing so, the bat clings to the thin branches that support the filaments of the web.

99

The biological and ecological significance of the habitat

With such a large number and variety of dwellings and roosts as has been described here, one cannot but gain the impression that finding a suitable hiding place in which to rest during the day must present no problem to bats. It seems that nature and man provide roosting sites in abundance. But the impression is a false one.

Most bats are unable to maintain a constant body temperature; it rises and falls in accordance with the ambient temperature. Therefore the temperature provided by the selected roost is very important for the daily activities of the bats. Temperature affects metabolism, and this in turn determines how "active" the bats are. Most bats function most effectively at temperatures of about 30°C. When the colder season of the year begins in our latitudes—usually the time when food also becomes scarce—the bats withdraw into frost-free winter quarters, reduce their metabolic rate considerably, and await the spring. More will be written of this interesting phenomenon in a later chapter.

In warmer regions it can also happen that the supply of food diminishes. In this case, the bats once again survive the critical period by finding a cooler place. The saving of energy by reduction of the metabolic rate and the resulting torpor can be observed even within the daily cycle. Many of the Free-tailed bats that live in rock crevices along coasts retreat to the furthest depths of these crevices in the morning. Since it is very cool there, they enter a state of lethargy which considerably retards metabolism. In the evening, they make their way to the opening of the crevices, warm themselves in the heat of the setting sun, and in this way, activate the metabolic process to such an extent that, within a short time, they are ready to set off on their flight in search of food.

Many bats exploit the different climatic conditions of the various localities within a house, so that they are able to organize the course of their life here throughout the entire year. The zoologist Gaisler of Brno describes how in summer the females in a colony of Lesser Horseshoe bats (*Rhinolophus hipposideros*) show a preference for the attics of houses. Here, the temperatures are usually higher and this is favourable for the development and rearing of young. Cool rainy days during the summer endanger the successful rearing of young bats. The situation is quite different for the males. They can afford to lower the energy balance and spend the day in a state of semi-torpor. So they are found in cooler parts of the house, for instance, under floorboards or even in the cellar. In autumn, depending on the temperature outdoors, females and young bats are found in various parts of the house. When winter comes, all the bats are re-united in the cellar where they roost in a dark, cool but frost-free situation. Similar observations have also been made of the Greater Horseshoe bat (*Rhinolophus ferrumequinum*) which, according to the season, is found in the various "storeys" of old castles.

In tropical regions, many species have principal and secondary sleeping quarters, although the day-time roosts show very constant temperatures. The secondary roosts are visited in particular when the bats are disturbed in their habitual quarters. Considerations of safety play a vital part in the selection of a roost. Branching and tortuous cave systems are much more advantageous and more sought-after than simple galleries.

It has been found that very large populations have several roosts at their disposal. For reasons that are not yet clear, the majority of the bats in the colony are found now in roost A, and then again in roost B or C. Thus, periodical assembling and dispersal takes place within such a colony of between 1000 and 100,000 individuals.

In this chapter, we have seen that bats live as solitary individuals or in large assemblies of various sizes, and that bats of the same sex sometimes group together in a particular roost. The latter phenomenon is exemplified in the maternity colonies. These are roosts in which female bats come together in order to give birth and rear their young.

As a generalization, it is clear that the majority of the many species of bats live a communal life. The Chiroptera are social creatures; solitary individuals are the exceptions. They are found at least in pairs, as is commonly the case among smaller species of fruit bats. But usually the pair consists not of male and female, but of mother and young. In almost all families, there are species that are less sociable and therefore found only in small groups. This may well be because the roost selected precludes the formation of a large congregation.

In temperate regions, where the females of most species form maternity colonies, the males adopt separate roosts, frequently close to the females. Since they live in small groups or as individuals and in addition are very secretive, they are difficult to find in the summer. There are also examples of totally male colonies.

In the tropics, maternity colonies are less usual. Here the entire social group, males, females and young, roost in the same place. Among Free-tailed bats *(Molossus)* and Tomb bats *(Taphozous)*, males and females are sometimes observed to form separate groups.

The fact that in the northern latitudes, the sexes live in separate quarters in the summer, while in the tropical zones, this habit is rare, can be observed even within a single species. For instance, the Horseshoe bat *Rhinolophus rouxi* of Northern India shows strict segregation of the sexes, whereas in Sri Lanka, males and females are always found together. In the case of some fruit bats of Northern India, the sexes live apart for a short period during the summer months. This phenomenon is not found in the same species living in tropical regions.

Little research has been carried out into the extent of competitive rivalry for territory and roosting sites. In the winter quarters in temperate zones, several species are often found together. For example, an annual total of more than 3000 bats overwintering in a chalk mine near Berlin includes Large Mouse-eared bats *(Myotis myotis)*, Daubenton's or Water bats *(Myotis daubentoni)*, Whiskered bats *(Myotis mystacinus)*, Natterer's bats *(Myotis nattereri)*, Long-eared bats *(Plecotus auritus)* and Pipistrelles *(Pipistrellus pipistrellus)*. In mine workings in Bohemia, ten different species have been observed in the winter. Usually, each individual species has its favourite roost, selected according to conditions of temperature and humidity. In the tropics, certain species share a common roosting site. This shows that the basic requirements determining the selection of living quarters are the same for many species, and that within these quarters, each species is very selective in its demands.

What bats eat

Diversity, such as we have met among bats in various fields so far, also characterizes the feeding habits of the Chiroptera. Although two major foods predominate —insects in the case of insectivorous bats (Microchiroptera) and fruits in the case of fruit bats (Megachiroptera)—various species have nevertheless become specialized in quite unexpected foods. This extension of the food spectrum shows that in the field of feeding, bats have once again been able to open up and occupy interesting new niches. In some cases, specialization has gone so far that certain species feed exclusively on blood or on pollen and nectar. On the other hand, no bat has adapted to an exclusive diet of grass or leaves. Clearly the energy gain from such a source is not sufficient for these flying mammals. The quantity of leaves or grass required to satisfy the requirements of bats would be too great, and its digestion would demand a considerably more voluminous intestinal tract, such as that of rodents or ungulates. The morphological adaptations involved would conflict with the bat's capacity for flight. But feeding on fruit presents no problems. The juicy flesh of fruit is rapidly digested and passes quickly through the intestines. Very often only the juice of the fruit is extracted and the fibrous matter rejected.

Insectivores

The majority of bats eat flying insects. Food of animal origin always has high nutritional value in comparison with the same volume of vegetable food. It can be consumed more rapidly and satisfies for a longer time. This last consideration is important for bats which must often go without food during the day for 14 to 18 hours.

The habit of feeding on insects led to the earlier subdivision of the order of Chiroptera into "insectivorous

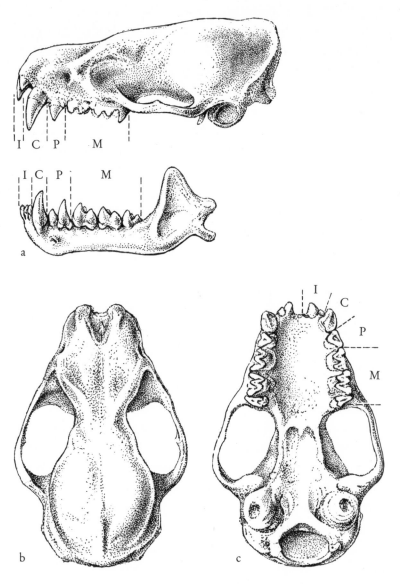

Skull of a Serotine *(Eptesicus serotinus)* seen from
a the side, b above and c below.
Dentition in the upper and lower jaw show absence or reduction of incisors and of premolars. The remaining teeth are well developed, pointed and in part knobby. They are reminiscent of the teeth of a beast of prey. The pointed canines seize the prey and the sharp molars grind down the chitinous shells of insects.
I incisors, C canines, P premolars, M molars.

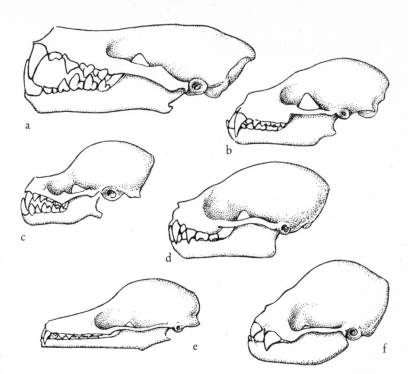

The adaptation of skull shape and dentition to different feeding habits in Spear-nosed bats and closely related Vampire bats (from Yalden and Morris, 1976)
a *Vampyrum*: small mammals, insects, fruits?,
b *Phyllostomus*: small mammals, insects, fruits,
c *Tonatia*: insects,
d *Artibeus*: fruits,
e *Anoura*: nectar and pollen,
f *Desmodus*: blood.
The insectivorous bats of the genus *Tonatia* show the least degree of specialization in dentition. The species *Vampyrum spectrum*, that lives mainly on small mammals, has large canines. As an adaptation to the blossom-visiting habit, the facial skull in *Anoura* is elongate and the teeth only weakly developed. The blood-feeding habit of the Common Vampire *(Desmodus)* makes chewing superfluous; the molars are greatly reduced. It is the function of the pointed, sharp incisors and canines to remove the hair covering at a suitable point on the body of the host animal and to make a small gash in the muscle from which blood will trickle.

bats" (Microchiroptera) and "fruit-eating bats" (Megachiroptera). In fact, every family of Microchiroptera—apart from Vampire bats—has representatives which feed on insects. But there are also fruit-eating members in some families of Microchiroptera. Insectivorous bats are found on every continent, and indeed in the temperate latitudes, the species are exclusively insectivorous. This form of feeding is undoubtedly the original, primitive one, since the Chiroptera are derived from insectivorelike stock. It was important for them to develop a system of location that would assist them in finding and seizing prey in the air, in the dark of night. With the evolution of ultrasonic echolocation, this problem was solved. Not only does it enable bats to find their way in the dark but it also directs them to a source of food. When bats came upon the scene, a new threat entered the life of the great host of nocturnal insects. From birds they had little to fear, for few birds hunt them at night, and during the day, when they are resting, their excellent protective coloration makes them virtually invisible. But for bats, they are major sources of food.

The precise hour of the evening at which bats set out on their nocturnal flight cannot be predicted. Differences exist between species, but even within a single species or even a single colony, variations can be observed from one day to the next. Clearly, the familiar "internal clock" controls the departure. Other influences in addition to meteorological factors may also be decisive, for example, the stage that has been reached in the rearing of young. It has been observed repeatedly that pregnant or lactating females start their flight rather earlier.

When colonies are small, the bats usually hunt in the vicinity of the day-time roost. Barbastelles *(Barbastella barbastellus)* are usually found within a radius of 500 m of the roost. Horseshoe bats *(Rhinolophus* spp.) also have a restricted range. However, if a colony consists of many thousands of bats, the hunting territory extends over ten kilometres or more. Species that do not find their food in the immediate vicinity of the roost make use of regular "flight paths" or "flyways" to reach their hunting area. As dawn breaks, they fly back along the same route to their roost.

Bats are not active continuously throughout the entire night. How long they are on the wing and how persistently they hunt depends to a great extent on the amount

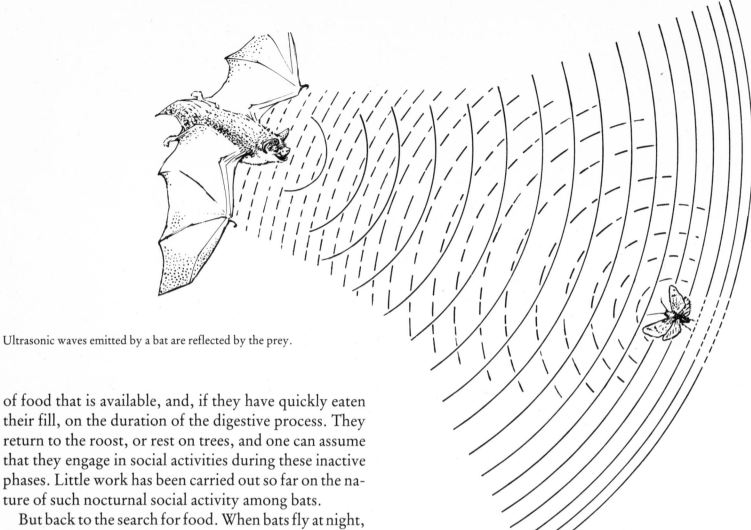

Ultrasonic waves emitted by a bat are reflected by the prey.

of food that is available, and, if they have quickly eaten their fill, on the duration of the digestive process. They return to the roost, or rest on trees, and one can assume that they engage in social activities during these inactive phases. Little work has been carried out so far on the nature of such nocturnal social activity among bats.

But back to the search for food. When bats fly at night, they emit short, regular sound pulses. The echoes that are bounced back provide the bats with information about obstacles in their flight path and about insects that are flying nearby. As soon as an insect is heard or enters the sound-sensing beam of a bat, the frequency of impulses is increased instantly to allow its exact location and pursuit. The noise produced, although inaudible to the human ear, registers an intensity greater than that of a pneumatic hammer.

Although the hunt for prey takes a different form in individual species, it always demands high manoeuvrability and almost acrobatic skill.

Common Noctules (*Nyctalus noctula*) and many tropical species of Free-tailed bats (Molossidae) ascend high into the air, in the manner of birds such as the swallow and the swift, and swoop down in plunging flight upon their prey. Pipistrelles (*Pipistrellus pipistrellus*) and

Serotines (*Eptesicus serotinus*), on the other hand, fly in rapid twisting flight, low down close to the ground. They like tree-covered or bushy terrain and so are frequently to be found in the parks and gardens of towns and villages. Other species such as the Daubenton's or Water bat (*Myotis daubentoni*) skim in low flight over the surface of fairly large bodies of water to catch the insects flying there. They have been observed also to catch those insects that run on the surface of the water.

The insects, of course, try to evade their pursuer. The bat, swooping at great speed, does not always succeed in catching the insect in its widely open mouth. So it will often try to draw the insect towards it with its wing tip, or to catch it in the interfemoral membrane and then take it into the mouth. The capture of an insect is made in the

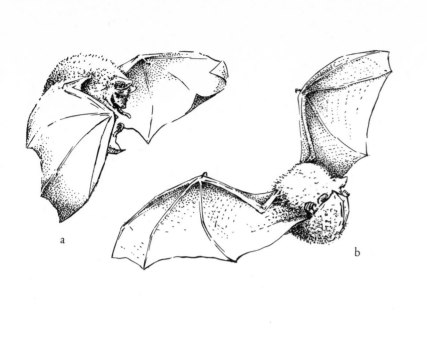
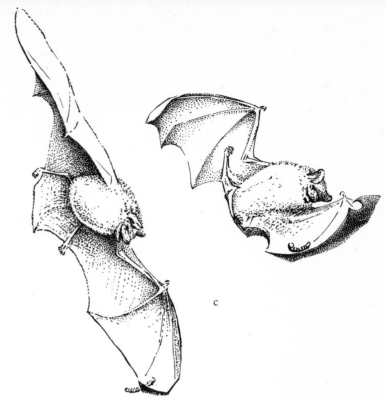

Variations on the capture of insect prey. Generally, small insects are seized directly with the mouth (a). Frequently bats catch larger insects initially in a "pouch" formed by the tail membrane then transfer it from there to the mouth (b). If the prey tries to escape, it is "seized" by the wing membrane and directed by a stroke towards the bat's head (c) (after Webster and Griffin, 1962).

fraction of a second. When the food supply is plentiful, the manoeuvre is repeated several times in a minute. If the insect that is caught is so large that it cannot be eaten on the wing, the bat repairs to a habitual feeding site where it roosts and consumes the "succulent" body of a moth or beetle, while the legs and wings are bitten off and allowed to fall to the ground.

Once an insect is held by the teeth of a bat, it has little prospect of escape. The dentition of this insectivore is reminiscent of that of a beast of prey. The large, needle-sharp, dagger-like canines pierce the prey and hold it fast, and the broad, intricately crenulated molars have no difficulty in chopping up the hard, chitinous body of an insect.

The size of the insect and the frequency of its wing beat are features which enable bats to distinguish between different species of insects when they are catching food. For the smaller species of bats, there is the added consideration that they are able to kill and eat only insects below a certain size. Since the different species of bats have specific hunting territories, and within these they pursue insects of a particular size, there is rarely any competition for food among the various bats in any one habitat.

The chitinous remains of the ectoskeletons of insects are only partially digested, and from an examination of the bat's excreta, it is possible to reconstruct its diet. In this way it was found that the Big Brown bat (*Eptesicus fuscus*) has a diet consisting of beetles (36%), hymenopterons such as bees, wasps and flying ants (26%), flies (13%), together with a small number of mayflies, caddis flies, stone flies and a few crickets and grasshoppers. A list of this kind is, of course, valid only for a particular region and a particular season of the year. The insect fauna in a different habitat during a different month could be quite dissimilar.

Moreover, food analysis of this kind is inevitably incomplete, since small insects are digested without leaving any identifiable remains. It is not merely by chance that beetles appear at the top of the list. Their hard wing covers are more readily preserved. They do not necessarily represent the major type of insect prey.

Phases of the flight manoeuvre in catching a mealworm tossed into the air (after Webster, 1967)

In examining the faeces of the Large Mouse-eared bat (*Myotis myotis*), the Bamberg zoologist Kolb found that during the entire summer half-year, these bats also include carabids (ground beetles) in their diet. If there is enough food of other kinds available, the proportion of carabids fluctuates. When cockchafers appear, they make up the greater part of the total food intake. In June, Kolb found large numbers of mole crickets, and when the mass flights of green oak-leaf rollers began, it was this moth which provided up to 90% of the food eaten by the Mouse-eared bats. In July, carabids came to the fore again and, for the sake of variety, grasshoppers were added to the menu. In autumn, it was found that a high proportion of dung beetles supplemented the diet of carabids. Clearly, demand is determined by supply.

There are many choice insects that can be caught by bats only with the greatest difficulty since they possess counterweapons. Some have developed silent flight which results from the existence of extremely fine hairs on every part of the body where air vortices could arise. In others, the body is enclosed in a soft, dense "fur" covering, which absorbs the sounds emitted by the bat, re-

turning only a weak echo. Many moths such as owlet moths, tiger moths and geometers are even capable of perceiving the bats from a considerable distance by means of their sense of hearing. In this case, the approaching bats betray themselves by their calls and cause the prey to take evasive action. Although the insects fly more slowly than their pursuers, they are usually able to escape with their life by a variety of strategic moves. Some drop to the ground like a stone, others set off in erratic zigzag flight which the bats cannot follow.

There are some moths which themselves emit a rapid succession of ultrasonic sounds when danger is most acute. But the noise is produced in quite a different way from that of bats. Rapid movements of the leg muscles cause vibrations in a chitinous plate situated where the hind legs join the body, which produces the sounds. The bats are irritated or frightened and give up the hunt.

Not all bats take their prey exclusively on the wing. They can also pick up non-flying insects from the ground. There have been reports that the African Slit-faced bat (*Nycteris thebaica*) picks up scorpions from the ground and eats them. According to investigations made by Kolb, Large Mouse-eared bats (*Myotis myotis*) can locate insects crawling on the ground. They fly towards them with unerring precision and track them down

among leaves or grass using their sense of smell. Experiments have shown that not all insects are acceptable as food. Mouse-eared bats could never be persuaded to accept potato (Colorado) beetles, either from the ground or in the air. Kolb was able to show that in the search for food, other species of bats also make use of their sense of smell in addition to their sense of hearing. From a distance of 10 to 20 cm, the bat's nose can tell it whether the creature being pursued is edible or not.

European Long-eared bats *(Plecotus)* are able to hover in the air like helicopters. This hovering flight, of which many raptors are also master, makes it possible for them to hover over foliage, tree trunks and walls of buildings and pick off insects, caterpillars and other creatures. All species of the Old and New World which pursue their food in this way show similar morphological modifications and adaptations.

Since the metabolism of small mammals is particularly high, and since in addition, flying requires a great deal of energy, bats are always voracious eaters. The great heaps of droppings under the roosts of their day-time quarters give some indication of the quantities of insects consumed by bats each night, namely, in small species something like half their body weight. Anyone who has ever kept bats in captivity knows that large species such as

the Large Mouse-eared bat and Common Noctule eat 30 to 40 mealworms a day or finish off 30 cockchafers in a very short time. Small Pipistrelles eat 40 to 50 flies in an hour. It is often difficult to provide them with a varied diet in such quantities. Therefore one cannot but advise in the strongest terms against keeping these useful animals simply as "pets", quite apart from the fact that it is illegal to keep protected animals in captivity. In addition to feeding, there are other necessities such as sleeping quarters and flight territory that can never be provided adequately for bats, so that sooner or later, captivity becomes a torment to them.

The following may serve to indicate the importance of the voracious appetite of these small mammals in the wild as an instrument of biological pest control. If a colony of 250,000 bats in which each individual weighs 15 to 20 g eats its fill in one night, it will have disposed of three to four tons of insects. Kolb estimated that during the mass flight of green oak-leaf rollers *(Tortrix viridana)*, the 800 Mouse-eared bats in a maternity colony in Bamberg destroyed a daily total of 55,000 of these insect pests. Clearly they are an important regulatory factor in maintaining the balance of nature, yet one which has almost completely lost its significance in industrial countries.

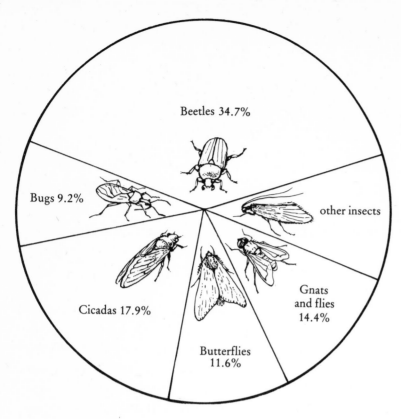

Beetles 34.7%

other insects

Bugs 9.2%

Gnats
and flies
14.4%

Cicadas 17.9%

Butterflies
11.6%

Dietary range of a cave-dwelling bat *(Myotis velifer)* from Kansas, U.S.A. Average quantities of insects consumed for the months of June to September

Fishing bats

It is difficult to imagine how bats that were originally exclusively insectivorous managed in a few rare cases to specialize in quite unusual foods. The opportunity to avoid competing with other bats for food by occupying the niche that offers fish as food, is one that has been taken by three species.

These species are not related to one another and live in quite different parts of the world. It may well be that their ancestors frequently caught insects from the surface of the water and from time to time scooped up a fish as well. The bat found this new food congenial and, from then on, gave it selective preference, until finally it became the sole source of food.

The best-known of the fish-eating bats is the Fisherman bat *(Noctilio leporinus)* of tropical America. In addition, the Vespertilionid *Pizonyx vivesi*, found in the Gulf of California and one species of *Myotis* in the Far East have also specialized in catching fish. Common to all of them are certain adaptations that enable them to secure their unusual food. In particular, the hind feet are exceptionally large and are furnished with strong claws. To catch a fish, the bats fly slowly, close to the surface of lakes or calm coastal waters. When they locate a fish, they snatch it up with their back feet and lift it from the water.

Bats are not natural swimmers and hardly ever enter water voluntarily. They have never been seen to submerge the entire body in water in order to seize a fish, as seabirds will do. Since fish often swim in large swarms close to the surface of water, there is usually no shortage of food. Difficulties in obtaining food arise only when strong wind and heavy rain whip up the water and make flying difficult. In captivity, a fish-eating bat has been found to consume 30 to 40 small fish in one night, a number that would be difficult to match in the wild. When the fish is caught, it is transferred by foot to the mouth, and if its size allows, is immediately eaten on the wing. Larger prey is held in the bat's mouth and carried to a roost, where it is eaten.

It is not yet known for certain how the fish are discovered and seized successfully. Ultrasonic echolocation undoubtedly enters into it, but clearly does not locate the fish itself, but rather the slight ripples produced by the fish on the surface of the water.

Bats that specialize in small vertebrates

In addition to fish, there are other vertebrates that serve as food for various bats. Certain Vespertilionids of tropical America have developed into regular carnivores. It is known that the Spear-nosed bat *(Phyllostomus hastatus)* likes to eat small rodents, other bats and small birds, in addition to fruit. The Giant Spear-nosed bat (*Vampyrum spectrum*) kills mice with ease. It is able to locate its prey in the rustling undergrowth and to seize the small rodents.

In the Old World, various representatives of the False Vampires or "cannibal bats" (Megadermatidae) are reported to pursue small rodents and eat them. Their diet also includes scorpions, frogs, birds and other bats. These specialist feeders among the Megadermatids land skilfully on the ground, and even with a comparatively heavy-bodied prey, are able to take off with great facility. They carry prey to a roost, where remnants of the meal can often be found in the form of skull and bone fragments.

In contrast to other groups of animals that are primarily carnivorous, no species of bat feeds on carrion. If bats are found close to carrion, it is undoubtedly because they are hunting for insects which are likely to be there.

It is estimated that about 70 per cent of all bats feed on insects and only 2 per cent feed exclusively on or supplement their diet by the addition of small vertebrates, which category, of course, includes fish.

Fruit-eating bats

The change from a diet of insects to mixed feeding or even to a diet consisting exclusively of vertebrates required less modification of the digestive system than did the adoption of a purely vegetable diet. This was a slow process of readjustment, resulting in many morphological changes. Probably at first these species ate a mixed diet of animal and vegetable food. Since many insects eat ripe fruit and their larvae live inside fruits, insectivorous bats looking for food were also attracted there. As they picked off the insects, no doubt they occasionally also bit off fragments of the sweet, juicy flesh of the fruit. It is palatable and the nutritional value is high, so increasing numbers of species in the tropics specialized in this new source of food and eventually became pure vegetarians. Of the Chiroptera living today, about a quarter are frugivorous.

The development of this kind of food specialization took place on two occasions in the bat kingdom, each quite independently of the other. It is interesting to see how the vegetarian feeders of the Old and of the New World went through similar (convergent) stages of development in their adaptation to a purely fruit diet. Special mention should be made here of the teeth, which are not pointed but have wide flat masticatory surfaces, and of the palate which is crossed by a series of ridges.

In the Old World, it is the numerous species within the family of the Megachiroptera which—equipped with a good memory for places and a sensitive nose—make their way with unerring precision to the trees of their feeding grounds, and have become specialists with an exclusively fruit diet. In the New World, there are many species of Spear-nosed bats (Phyllostomidae) that exploit this potential food source. But this family also includes many insectivorous species. The fruit eaters among the Spear-nosed bats have an equally good sense of smell, but they find their way about, as do all the Microchiroptera, by means of ultrasonic echolocation.

In both the Old and the New World, certain species of fruit bats have specialized in frequenting flowers, and feed on pollen and nectar. They will be examined in more detail in the next chapter.

All frugivorous bats inhabit the tropics. In densely forested regions, the vegetation is so luxuriant and varied that throughout the entire year there are trees and shrubs bearing ripe fruit. In the darkness, the bats are guided to the aromatic, sweet and succulent fruits by their sensitive organ of smell. Originally, fruit bats fed only on wild fruits. With the increasing cultivation of bananas, figs, guavas, mangoes, oranges and grapefruit, the bats turned their attention with enthusiasm to these fruits also. In the course of a night, they easily consume an amount equal to their own body weight. Consequently, fruit bats can cause considerable damage to fruit crops in certain areas. To protect their plantations, the farmers tried to exterminate the bats. Their meagre success did not justify the expense and effort. It proved much more satisfactory to harvest the fruit before it had ripened.

The fruit bats and fruit-eating Spear-nosed bats consume some kinds of fruit whole, others they crush in the mouth and swallow the juice together with a little of the fruit pulp. The broad-surfaced teeth and the tongue, which compress the fruit against the ridged palate, are equipment well suited for the purpose of extracting nourishing juices. The bats spit out the fibrous matter that cannot be crushed. Their food, then, consists entirely of water and sugars. The great length of intestine usual and indeed essential in herbivores is not necessary. They do not require a host of bacteria to break down copious cellulose components. Observations of bats in captivity have shown digestion in fruit-eating bats to be such a rapid process that urine is excreted within a very short time of feeding.

The ecological significance of feeding habits

A particular biotope can provide food for only a certain number of individuals. Therefore it is utilized to the full. Even where an adequate supply of food is available, some degree of "division of labour" ensures that all the reserves within the biotope are exploited. An example of this is the way in which certain species specialize in hunting for food close to the surface of water, others along the margins of woods or avenues of trees, others again high above the tree tops. Even the insects on leaves and in the ground cover are included. In the tropics, particularly on islands, it has been found that in terms of diet, the composition of species shows quite typical distribution groups. For example, a particular area was inhabited by two fruit-eating species, two nectar-feeding species, two insectivorous species and one fish-eating species. Each species has its special food categories and hunting zones, and scarcely impinges upon the territory of others.

In many places, the feeding habits of bats are an important factor in maintaining the balance of nature. In the sphere of biological pest control, the destruction of insect pests by insectivorous bats, particularly where the bats occur in large colonies, has an importance which should not be underestimated.

The frugivorous species, on the other hand, play an important part in the distribution of tropical plants. Since they frequently carry off fruits and eat them on trees in the surrounding area, they also effect the dispersal of the seeds. It can be seen that many plants have adapted to the distribution of their seeds by bats. Their fruits are long-stemmed and when ripe, remain hanging on the branch for a considerable time. In addition, they give off an aroma that attracts the bats at night. Moreover, not all tropical plants bloom and bear fruit at the same time. If they did so, the fruit-eating Chiroptera would have no food at certain seasons of the year, and moreover, the excess of food at other seasons would diminish the chances for seed dispersal by bats for many species of trees and bushes.

The relationship between bat and plant is one of mutual advantage and profit. A true symbiosis exists between the two.

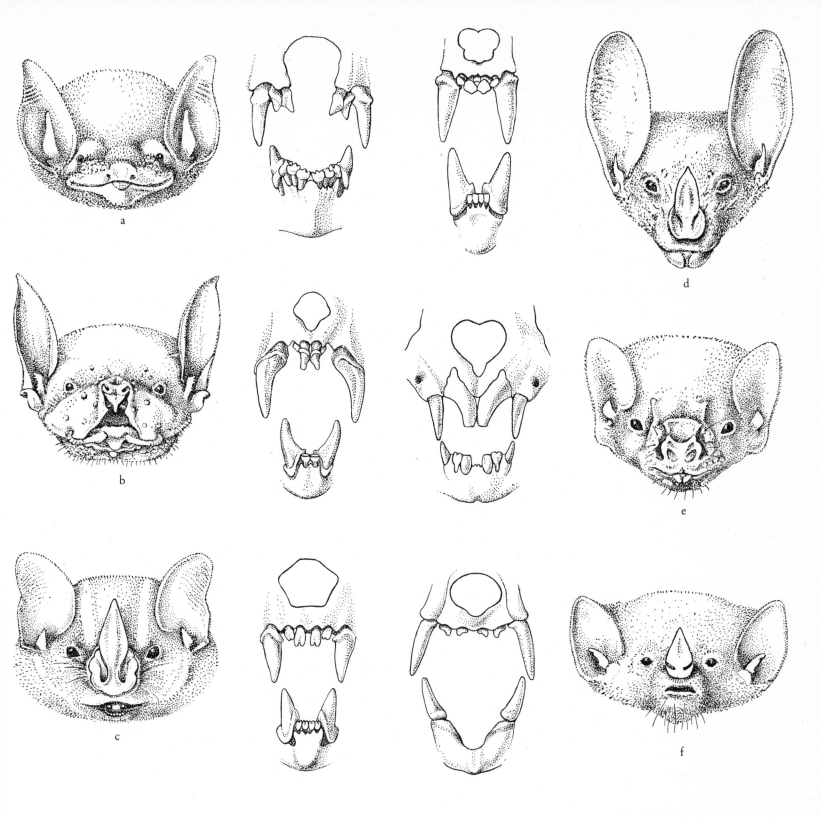

Sketches of various species of bats illustrating the effect of diet on the development of incisors and canines (based on Husson, 1962)

a *Myotis nigricans*: insects   b *Noctilio leporinus*: fish
c *Uroderma bilobatum*: fruits   d *Vampyrum spectrum*: small mammals
e *Diaemus youngi*: blood   f *Lichonycteris obscura*: nectar and pollen

Bat flowers and flower bats

Many flowering plants, in the extremely critical phase of pollination, depend entirely upon animals and moreover, animals capable of flight. Over the course of millions of years diverse and sometimes highly specialized relationships have developed between plant and animal. Not only have plants continually evolved new forms, colours, scents and even behaviour patterns, but in addition, many animals have adapted in various ways to the habit of frequenting blossoms. It is well known that bees, flies and butterflies as well as African sunbirds and South American humming-birds feed on the nectar of plants, and in doing so, pollinate those plants. Not many people are aware that there are also certain bats that feed on blossoms.

In flowering plants, the male generative cells, in the form of pollen, cannot make their way actively to the ova to fertilize them. Another means of transfer had to be found. Nature has solved the problem in three ways, making use of the mobility of three transfer media to carry the pollen. These are wind, water and animals that can fly.

So we distinguish between plants that are pollinated by wind action (anemophilous), those pollinated by water action (hydrophilous) and those by the action of animals (zoidiophilous). By comparing different blossoms, it soon becomes clear, even to the non-expert, to which type a flower belongs. The wind-pollinated blossoms have no need to attract attention; their blossoms are small and their colours restrained. Usually they are not at all conspicuous. Scarcely anyone notices the blossom of poplars, birches or alder trees. The blossoms of those plants pollinated by the action of animals are of quite a different kind, being large and striking in colour and scent. They are the ones that are really thought of as flowers. These flowers can consist of a single blossom, as tulips do, or can be an entire inflorescence, as is, for example, the sunflower.

The flower has the function of drawing attention and attracting and it takes on different forms according to which animals visit that particular plant. Insects and birds are wooed by visual stimuli. In addition, the fragrance of many flowers has an effect on insects, and in the case of certain tropical plants, on bats as well. Since bats are active only at night, this is when the blossoms open. Brilliance of colouring would be of no account at night, so the blossoms of chiropterophile flowers are inconspicuous in colouring.

Animals that visit blossoms do not fly there for the sake of the attractive colours or scents, but in search of food. If they found none, even the most beautiful flowers would lose their interest and would no longer be frequented. Usually the animals do not come in vain, but find sweet-tasting nectar, rich in carbohydrates, and in addition, pollen that is a valuable source of protein. Nectar alone, with a sugar content of 17 to 20 per cent—the rest is water—could not maintain the strength of the bats. They must also eat pollen in order to obtain the protein they need. It has been found that the pollen of chiropterophile flowers contains proportionally much more protein than the pollen of other flowers (agave, for example, 43 per cent).

Flowers visited by birds and bats provide much more nectar than those frequented only by insects. The American zoologist Howell was able to collect up to half a cup of nectar from a single inflorescence of many bat flowers. Even this amount of food is not sufficient to satisfy a bat. It is necessary for the creatures to visit many flowers every day to assuage their hunger.

It is an advantage to the plant that the individual blossoms contain only small quantities of nectar, since this necessitates visits to further blossoms, by which means the vital transfer of pollen is effected. The cunningly shaped and arranged anthers and stigmas inside the blossoms ensure that the pollen will adhere to parts of the body of the visiting animal that will come into contact with the reproductive organs at the next blossoms, and deposit pollen there. Pollination thus achieved is an important recompense to the plant for food supplied to its guests.

In order to obtain nectar from the tubular blossoms, many insects have evolved a long proboscis. Flower birds such as the humming-birds or Hawaiian honeycreepers possess long, thin beaks and a highly protrusible tongue with a brush-like tip. Adaptations of a similar kind are found in the bats that visit flowers. Extension of the facial skull and a very long, protrusible tongue are typical characteristics of a flower bat. On the other hand, the molar teeth are greatly reduced.

For much fascinating information on bat-pollinated plants and the reciprocal adaptations in flower and bat, we are indebted to the botanist Vogel. On his travels in South America, he discovered a large number of species of plants that are visited by bats. These were not only woody plants but also epiphytes and cactus plants.

Vogel was able to show that in Central and South America, the geographical distribution of plants that are pollinated by bats coincides to a large extent with the distribution of bat species that frequent blossoms. Their range extends northwards to the southern states of the U.S.A. (Texas, Arizona). Here, various species of cactus and agave are visited by bats. Most of the bats in question are glossophagine Nectar or Long-nosed bats *(Leptonycteris nivalis* and *L. sanborni)* and Mexican Long-tongued bats *(Choeronycteris mexicana)*. These species occur here only as summer visitors, at the time when the bat flowers blossom. In South America, bat plants occur south of northern Argentina. Here, the Long-tongued bat *(Glossophaga soricina)* and the Pale Spear-nosed bat *(Phyllostomus discolor)* are the species that can be seen most frequently visiting blossoms. A similar correlation in the geographical distribution of bat flowers with that of flower-visiting bats was also established in Southeast Asia.

The first indications of bats visiting flowers are of comparatively recent date. Apart from sporadic statements made at about the turn of the century, it was not until the thirties that reports drew attention to the flower-visiting habits of bats in Southeast Asia, Africa and Central America. There were repeated reports of small bats having been found feeding in the flowers of the African baobab tree *(Adansonia digitata)*. And in botanical gardens in Central America, small bats were again observed flying round baobab trees. The vital importance of bats in the propagation of these trees was illustrated in Hawaii. Numbers of baobab trees that were introduced here remained infertile because there were no bats to pollinate them.

One of the first trees to be recognized as a tree visited by bats, because of the shape of its blossom, was the calabash trees *(Crescentia* spp.)

Blossom-visiting by bats was at first presented as a curiosity. Up to that time, few people were prepared to believe that bats could feed on nectar and pollen. It seemed much more likely that the bats were visiting the flowers to catch the many insects flying round them.

The details of a bat's visit to a flower are difficult to capture, even using modern techniques. The event takes place only under the cloak of darkness, and moreover, usually in the tops of trees in tropical forests. Therefore in the case of many plants that are assumed to be pollinated by the action of bats (chiropterophile), ultimate proof of this—namely the observed visit of a bat to the blossom of these plants—still eludes us today. Frequently, the only indication of the visitor is the impression left on the petals by the claw of the thumb.

113

Many bat-pollinated plants facilitate their guest's visit in various ways. They have long-stemmed, large flowers that extend beyond the canopy of leaves; in others, the flowers lie close up against the trunk. Some plants shed their leaves when they bloom, and as a result, the bats can reach the blossom more easily. The inconspicuous colours of the blossoms vary between greenish-white, dull red, dingy brown and inky blue. Usually they open in the evening, shortly before or after darkness has fallen and often blossom only for a single night.

Many of the blossoms exude a "fragrance" that is difficult to describe; it has been called unpleasantly stale-smelling, cabbage-like and also musky. Others give off an odour of fermenting, over-ripe fruit; some of the species that visit them have evolved from fruit-eating species. The number of species of plants in the tropics that show specialization in pollination by bats contrasts with the considerably smaller number of species of bats that visit blossoms.

It is interesting to note that specialization in nectar and pollen feeding has taken place both in the Old and in the New World, quite independently of one another. In Africa and Asia, there are some 15 species of fruit bats belonging to the group of Long-tongued Fruit bats (Macroglossinae) and in America, about 40 members of the Spear-nosed bats, namely the Nectar-feeding Small Spear-nosed bats (Phyllonycterinae) and the Nectar-feeding Phyllostomids (Glossophaginae) that successfully occupy this niche. Also a number of Stenodermine Spear-nosed bats feed partly at flowers and partly at fruit.

Since not all bat plants blossom throughout the year, and certain differences in form exist among blossoms, the bats use various techniques to obtain nectar. They hover in the air in front of many of the flowers and insert only the tongue and tip of the snout; on other blossoms,

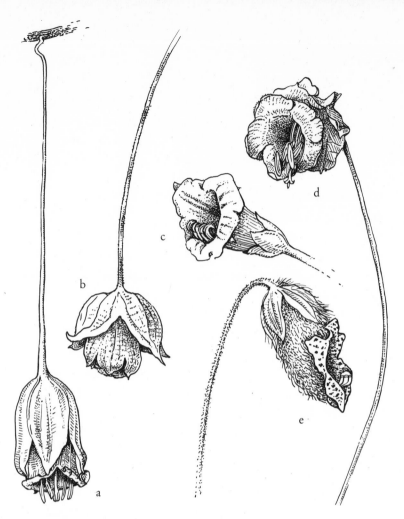

Long-stemmed flowers of plants pollinated by bats (chiropterophile) in South America (after Vogel, 1958)
a *Trianacea speciosa* (Solanaceae)
b *Cayaponia* sp. (Cucurbitaceae)
c *Symbolanthus latifolius* (Gentianaceae)
d *Cobaea scandens* (Polemoniaceae)
e *Campanea grandiflora* (Gesneriaceae).

they take a firm hold first of all with the claws of the thumbs or back legs, and then extract nectar and pollen. At the moment of drinking, the extended wings are motionless. After no more than one or two seconds, the bats allow themselves to fall, and fly away. They circle the tree briefly, and quick as a flash, fly to another blossom. Apart from short intervals, the flower bats are active in this way the entire night.

The visit of a Pale Spear-nosed bat *(Phyllostomus discolor)* to blossoms of the tree *Parkia auriculata* that is distributed throughout the world, is described by Vogel in

114

the following way. The inflorescences, that consist of three blossom kinds (generative, nectar and scent blossoms), are approached diagonally from below. Suddenly, the bats throw themselves round so that they can grasp hold with the back legs. The thumb plays no part in this. The wings are held extended and almost motionless. Head and neck curve round the lower, fertile flower head, so that the mouth approaches the nectar ring from below. It is licked clean in less than a second with the brush-like tip of the tongue. Then the bat draws back its head sharply, relinquishes its hold and flies diagonally downwards and away. Inadvertently it has brushed against the generative blossoms with its cheek, neck and belly, and pollinated them. The Short-nosed bats, which in India regularly visit the blossoms of the baobab tree, also hold on to the blossoms with their back feet and in addition, the claw of the thumb grips the upper part of the blossom. The weight of the bat bends the stem and blossom over; this causes the nectar to flow on to the lower petal from which it can easily be licked. In this way, even those species that are primarily fruit eaters and show no special adaptations in the region of the head to nectar feeding, can reach the precious food deep inside the blossom.

Many blossoms possess a deep calyx into which the bat must insert not only the entire head but also the shoulders, in order to obtain the sweet nectar.

The true flower bats are very small members of the Chiroptera. Both the Macroglossinae (Long-tongued Fruit bats) and the Glossophaginae (Nectar-feeding Phyllostomids) are among the smallest species of their families.

Since most of the fruit bats are of a quite impressive size, the nectar-feeding species, with a body only 6 to 7 cm in length, appear like dwarfs among giants. They have the advantage that they can adapt more easily to nectar feeding.

The adaptations described above, which animal and plant have undergone in order to develop this mutually beneficial cooperation, are the result of millions of years of evolution. It may well be that some of the nectar-feeding bats proceeded directly from feeding on insects, with which many species still supplement their diet, to feeding on nectar, whereas other species specialized in feeding on fruit first. Some fruit bats have been observed to consume petals as well. In such cases, they destroy the blossom and damage the plant.

The Indian Short-nosed or Dog-faced Fruit bat (Cynopterus sphinx) is said to be partial to the honey-sweet blossoms of the banana tree, and to cause widespread damage in many plantations. The Banana bat (Musonycteris harrisoni), discovered in Mexico only 20 years ago, on the other hand, lives exclusively on the nectar of the banana blossoms.

In the case of bat flowers and flower bats, a high degree of specialization brings mutual advantage to the partners involved. The situation is quite different in the adaptation of certain bats to blood feeding. The adoption of this source of food is true parasitism, unique among mammals. But of this, more in the next chapter.

Vampires—fable and fact

The picture of a vampire that most people hold in their imagination is only partially realized by the true Vampire bats. Their specialization in a diet of blood, that is, their habit of "sucking" blood or, rather more accurately, of drinking blood, is undoubtedly somewhat repugnant. But in their external appearance, they do not show such grotesque features as many other species of bats. And in the Old World and the New, it was other bats that came to be represented as vampires and still today reflect this fact in their names, the False Vampire (*Megaderma spasma*) and *Vampyrum spectrum* (the Giant Spear-nosed bat). Both were reputed to suck blood. And so they combined all the characteristics necessary to enable them to play the leading role in any tale of horror. Few other mammals have inspired in the human imagination such a combination of terror, respect and fascination as have "vampires".

What then are the plain facts about the true Vampires (Desmodontidae), about that family of bats whose members feed exclusively on the blood of vertebrates? It is certainly the most extreme example of food specialization among the Chiroptera. As a consequence, Vampire bats have become the only parasites among mammals. Not only this particular adaptation, unique among vertebrates, but also economic problems that have resulted from it in recent decades have made the Vampire bat the focus of particular interest.

Apart from the fruit-eating species of bats that from time to time do some damage to fruit plantations, true Vampires are the only members of the Chiroptera that cause extensive and serious harm to man. The three known species live exclusively in the New World. They have evolved from the large family of Spear-nosed bats. The best-known and most widely researched representative of the Vampire bats is the Common Vampire (*Desmodus rotundus*). Like the other two species, it inhabits tropical and subtropical regions of America, from Mexico to northern Chile and Argentina. Vampire bats are relatively small, with a body length of about 7 cm, and they weigh about 30 g. The fur is reddish-brown above with lighter, yellowish-brown underparts. They have no tail and the interfemoral membrane is correspondingly narrow. The head is short and rounded with relatively large eyes and a broad nose, with a fleshy nose leaf. The snout is compact, with a rather pig-like appearance. An indication of their feeding habits, in addition to the deeply grooved lower lip, is the abnormal dentition, in which the number of teeth is greatly reduced. In contrast to insectivorous species of bats that have up to 36 teeth, *Desmodus* has only 22. A diet of blood has rendered teeth superfluous, with the vital exception of the upper incisors and canines. These are very large, razor-sharp and set well forward. With them, the bat inflicts a shallow wound in the skin of its victim, through which the blood can trickle. The notched lower lip is pressed against the wound and blood is lapped up, using the tongue. For their attack, Vampire bats select those areas of their victim's body that are well supplied with blood, and where the skin is thin. *Desmodus* will usually bite large hoofed animals on the neck, the ears or the legs. When the victim is a human, the bat will, if possible, slash the big toe. The White-winged Vampire (*Diaemus youngi*) prefers feeding on the blood of birds. The victims are bitten on the neck or more commonly on the joints of the leg or the anal region.

Little is known of the habits of the third species, the Hairy-legged Vampire (*Diphylla ecaudata*). It is said to feed on the blood of birds rather than that of mammals.

An anticoagulant in the bat's saliva introduced into the wound prevents clotting of the blood. As a result, bleeding can persist for hours. Since the victims of the Vampire bat's attacks are usually large mammals that spend the night at rest, a system of echolocation is of less importance than it is to insectivorous species. In seeking out their source of food, the bats depend much more upon their relatively large eyes and acute sense of smell.

Although the first reports of "blood-sucking" bats reached Europe in the sixteenth century, it was only in the present century that these species gained such importance. In comments on the subject of Vampire bats written in 1857 by Kolenati in his *Naturgeschichte der Europäischen Chiropteren* (Natural History of the Chiroptera of Europe), the author was still able to say that "many of the evil reports of this notorious bloodsucker are without foundation". It was, of course, well known that they bite horses and pack animals, and take blood from them, but it was thought that this was probably owing to lack of insect food. Serious illness or death due to Vampires had never been established.

The situation changed when cattle breeding became increasingly extensive in many countries of Central and South America. Growing numbers of cattle herds provided these specialist feeders with a welcome addition to their list of potential hosts. Conditions were favourable for an increase of their own population.

In the early thirties, an epidemic of rabies broke out in Trinidad, which, within a short time, claimed 89 human victims and carried off thousands of cattle. It was recognized that Vampire bats had spread the fatal virus. Suddenly they were the centre of universal interest.

It is not clear how these specialized feeders evolved. Perhaps certain species of bats originally lived mainly on blood-feeding insects, and frequently would find them sitting on various mammals and birds, until finally they themselves began to lick blood directly from the wounds of the host.

Detailed investigations have shown that Vampire bats frequent all known domestic animals, that is, cattle, horses, goats, pigs as well as domestic poultry. They approach dogs more rarely, probably because these animals are more alert to attack. There are many reports of sleeping humans, particularly children, having been bitten. If bats are given the opportunity to select from a wide range of prey, they are found to prefer certain types of animals, even particular breeds. But it is not the taste of the blood that determines the preference, but the behaviour pattern characteristic of that species or breed. Colour of hide or details of the anatomical structure of the skin may also serve as criteria of choice. According to the zoologist Turner, calves are bitten more often than cows, because their periods of sleep are longer.

Vampire bats are very wary and leave their roost only under the darkness of night. Their period of activity reaches a peak before midnight and again soon after midnight, provided there is no moon. On bright, moonlit nights no Vampire bats are to be seen. They do not leave their roosts, in order, many workers believe, to avoid certain nocturnal raptors that are their natural enemies. However, detailed research carried out by Turner into the habits and behaviour of Vampires, shows that they have other reasons for not appearing on moonlit nights. On light nights, many animals at pasture move about as they graze, and it is not possible for the bats to draw blood from their victims. But when it is quite dark, they fly low across the ground in small groups, searching for their prey. Usually they circle above them several times before landing. Earlier writers also observed this circling action and wove phantastic tales from it. It was said that Vampires would hover on the wing in front of the cow's face, until the victim fell into a hypnotic sleep and so did not notice the blood-letting. Undoubtedly, Vampires set to work with insidious care once they have selected a victim, but they do not use hypnosis. They approach without the slightest sound, select a suitable area for attack and slash the skin so rapidly that the sleeping victim, man or animal, is not even wakened. Travellers who have spent the night in the open without adequate protection have reported that they did not even realize until next morning that they had been attacked by Vampire bats. Blood stains showed where the bats had struck. Since the wounds were made painlessly, the victims had not even been roused from sleep.

This manner of obtaining food makes it essential for Vampires to be agile, not only in the air but also on the ground. They can walk and run more nimbly than other bats, and hop forwards and backwards like small hobgoblins. These characteristics are extremely useful as they approach their prey, and equally so if they are disturbed and must make off rapidly. As they alight on the host, small soft pads of skin on the joints of the hand and soles of the feet cushion the impact. Once the landing has been effected, the body is held well above the surface with only the soft soles of the feet touching the host.

Often Vampires land at some distance from their victim and creep or hop cautiously towards it. Up to fourteen bats have been observed simultaneously on one horse, and a host animal may be bitten more than thirty times in one night. Usually each bat taps its own source. If the blood flows strongly, several bats will lick at one wound. Frequently a number of different bats will visit the same bite in turn. The length of time spent on the host varies greatly, and can be up to 40 minutes.

If the Vampire is allowed to feed undisturbed, it will gorge until its body seems ready to burst and it has difficulty in launching into flight. Sometimes it must wait for a while after feeding until it is able to fly again. Until then, it will creep into some nearby shelter, taking advantage of its agility on the ground.

Laboratory experiments have shown that a Common Vampire consumes 15 to 20 millilitres of blood in a day. This represents almost 40 per cent of its body weight. In the wild, the bat will probably consume more nearly its

own weight in blood. Because blood has a high water content, quantities of this magnitude are needed to satiate the bat. From these figures, it can be concluded that a Vampire takes about 7 litres of blood in a year, and a colony of 100 bats consumes a quantity of blood equal to that of 25 cows or 14,000 hens.

The structure of the bat's stomach is adapted to this manner of feeding. Not only is it long and coiled, but also extraordinarily expansible. Similar adaptations are found in other blood-feeding animals. When Vampires are satiated, they fly back to their day-time roosts, from which they may not emerge until several days later.

Vampires roost either as solitary individuals or in colonies of thousands in old buildings, dark caves and hollow trees. They often share a roosting site with other species of bats. When they return from feeding they devote themselves to a lengthy thorough grooming. The feet are used to clean the fur; flight membranes and thumbs are licked clean by the tongue.

The bite of the Vampire is in itself harmless, and any healthy mammal can withstand a single blood-letting with no difficulty whatsoever. But the general health of an animal can be affected if it is bitten repeatedly. In addition, flies and other insects often lay their eggs in the open wounds caused by Vampires. Serious infection can result. Grazing animals are debilitated and can become worthless. But by far the greatest danger that threatens man and animal is that the Vampires can spread dangerous diseases as they feed. They are greatly feared in the countries of tropical America as transmitters of disease. In addition to tetanus in cattle and an infectious disease fatal to horses, the major disease they spread is rabies.

The leaping capacity of Vampire bats is unique among the Chiroptera. They hop forwards, sideways or backwards like small hobgoblins. In this way, they are able to approach their victims stealthily or to evade them skilfully (sketches after photographs from Leen, 1976).

The incubation period for rabies is about two weeks in Vampires. For some of them, it is fatal, but others survive apparent exposure.

Rabies, transmitted by Vampire bats, threatens whole herds of cattle in Latin America, where it has become a serious veterinary and medical problem. Not the "false vampires" of the horror films but the true Vampires are the ones which, as it has turned out, have given many people sleepless nights. Recent estimates put the annual loss of cattle at a million head, representing a sum of more than 100 million dollars.

In 1966, the World Health Organization decided to send in a team of experts to deal with the problem. The initial measures included the vaccination of large numbers of livestock, but this brought little success. More important were the attempts to combat the transmitters of the disease. The authorities in the U.S.A. began to work out a long-term programme with the aim of recording vampire numbers and distribution, in order to analyze their habits and from the findings, to work out measures of control. Only when more was known about the preferred roosts, the numbers in the colonies and their methods of finding and taking food, reproductive patterns and social behaviour, and the influence of the weather on flight activity, would it be possible to introduce effective measures of control.

Meanwhile, the farmers took action of their own. They tried to destroy the Vampires in their roosts, using dynamite, gas and poison sprays. The widespread but uncoordinated vigilante activity of the cattle farmers did little to reduce the numbers of Vampires; they did, however, succeed in endangering and even destroying many other species of bat.

An American zoologist Greenhall, who had studied the vampire problem for decades, developed a method in which strychnine syrup was placed on the wound. If the Vampire returned to that particular wound, it would ingest the poison along with blood. It proved possible to exterminate a fairly large number of Vampire bats in this way, but success was only partial. Similarly, attempts at shooting or netting Vampire bats brought only temporary respite.

After years of practical research, American scientists developed a substance that causes the death of Vampires by internal bleeding. The anticoagulant, called Diphenadion, is injected into the bloodstream of grazing cattle in small quantities that are harmless to them. But when the substance is swallowed by Vampires as they drink the blood, it causes weakening of the vascular walls and internal bleeding. Coagulation of the blood is prevented and the bats die within two or three days.

On experimental farm stations, where the substance was first tested, there was a distinct decline in the number of fresh bites within a very short time. One great advantage of this material is its long-term effectiveness, since re-injection of the grazing cattle need be carried out only after three to five years.

A second method of dealing with Vampire bats exploits their strongly marked grooming instincts. An ointment again containing an anticoagulant is spread on the fur and wing membranes of Vampire bats that have been caught in nets. The bats are set free and return to their roosts, where they start the extensive process of grooming. This involves licking the fur of other bats, and ensures that many other Vampires also come in contact with the substance and are destroyed. In field tests, 6 bats from a colony of sixty living in a cave were caught, ointment was applied and the bats liberated. Checks made after one week showed that only one bat was still alive in this cave.

The measures of control are organized in such a way that they do not cause the indiscriminate destruction of all Vampires, but merely regulate the size of the bat population. This is essential in areas of intensive cattle farming. Even though all the methods so far developed still have certain drawbacks, chemical control is still a means of providing valuable help to the cattle farmers of tropical America.

The specialization of Vampire bats in blood feeding has shown how this otherwise insignificant creature can, as a result of particular circumstances, become an unexpectedly important economic factor within its area of distribution.

These efforts made to control Vampire bats emphasize how vitally important it is to study in detail the way of life and habits of every animal. Only then is it possible to regulate a population effectively on occasions when the balance of nature is disturbed.

"Seeing" with sound

There is no doubt that the development of a system of ultrasonic echolocation has been of great advantage to bats. Strictly speaking, it is only the Microchiroptera, the "insectivorous" bats, that have this perfect sensory capability at their disposal. The fruit bats (Megachiroptera) use visual orientation. A single exception is that of the cave-dwelling bats of the genus *Rousettus*. In addition to visual orientation, they also possess a well-developed ultrasonic direction-finding system, which they have evolved quite independently of the ultrasonic orientation of the Microchiroptera. In these bats, visual and acoustic systems support and supplement each other. When they return to their day roosts after their feeding flights, they switch from visual orientation to echolocation.

Bats are able to produce a wide range of vocal sounds that are also perceptible to the human ear. If bats are startled from sleep or if they disturb one another, high shrill sounds can often be heard, which can be described as twittering, whining or shrieking. These vocal sounds can also be heard in the reproductive season, as the sexes attract or pursue one another.

But this chapter is concerned with those sounds that human ears do not perceive, since they are in the ultrasonic range.

Making use of ultrasonic echolocation, bats conquered nocturnal air space and a whole new feeding area, to an extent that would have been impossible with visual orientation alone. Now they were in a position to track down the great army of nocturnal insects, even very small species, by making use of their ears. They were virtually in sole command of this abundant food supply.

The use of a system of echolocation is not exclusive to bats. Other animals make use of the same principle, although not to such a great extent, nor with such a degree of perfection. Shrews, for instance, find their way by means of ultrasonic emissions, and various species of toothed whales make use of echolocation in the ocean, in order to detect animal prey and avoid obstacles. It became known about thirty years ago that certain birds, such as the guacharo or oil-bird (*Steatornis*), which is related to the nightjars, found in the north of South America, and the cave swiftlets (*Aerodromus* spp., formerly included in the genus *Collocalia*) of the order of swifts (Apodiformes) in Southeast Asia and Australia, are able to find their way by a system of echolocation. In contrast to our bats, the pitch of the sounds used by these birds, at about 10 kHz, is within the limits audible to the human ear. Accuracy of the auditory image is not very great. For guacharos and cave swiftlets, as for *Rousettus* fruit bats, echolocation plays little part in the acquisition of food. However, it allows the creatures to colonize underground quarters where no light penetrates. Here they nest in colonies of several thousand individuals, and use their "click" sounds to locate their roosting places. Even though they have large eyes that function in very dim light (scotopic vision), these alone would not enable them to make their way into roosts of this kind. Moreover, the birds use their sense of sight in seeking food, whereas the fruit bats also rely on their sense of smell.

It was only very recently that man was able to solve the mystery of how bats can move about with such assurance and to seek out and catch their prey in the darkest of nights. For 50 million years, they have had their own system of ultrasonic transmitters, direction finders and "radar" equipment, while man has been able to develop these technological aids only in the last few decades and with a vast expenditure of time and energy.

There has been no lack of attempts to discover the secret of the bat's capacity for nocturnal flight. Some of the earliest theories put forward were on the right lines, but it required the sophisticated apparatus of modern scientific practice to provide an explanation of this amazing achievement of the animal senses.

For many people, an explanation was easily found: these sinister "birds" that fly so confidently in the dark, catching even quite tiny insects, must be in possession of magic powers—undoubtedly they are the devil's own creatures.

At the end of the eighteenth century, an Italian naturalist and priest, Lazzaro Spallanzani, in defiance of his superstitious contemporaries, made the first attempt to lay this particular ghost. In his experiments on nocturnal animals, he found that an owl could fly across his room in half-light with no difficulty. But if his room was in total darkness, the owl blundered helplessly into every obstacle. When he repeated these experiments with bats, he discovered to his astonishment, that even in total darkness, they were able to avoid all obstacles in his study, as surely as if they could see them. In addition, he hung threads across the length and breadth of his room, but the result was the same: at no time did the bats strike them. However, when Spallanzani covered the head of each bat with a small hood of opaque material, they suddenly blundered against walls and fell to the ground. From this, he drew the conclusion that bats find their way visually, and obviously can do so even with exceedingly small amounts of light.

It might well have seemed that the problem was solved. However, Spallanzani carried out further experiments and discovered that covering or even removing the bat's eyes had no effect on the powers of orientation.

When the Swiss zoologist Jurine learned about this work, he added one more decisive experiment to the series. He plugged the ears of bats and found that their sense of direction failed. Spallanzani repeated these experiments many times and obtained the same result: bats require their sense of hearing in order to find their way.

But who at that time would believe such an assertion? Nobody was able to detect any sound, so proof of orientation by means of sound could not be furnished. In addition, the renowned and influential French naturalist Cuvier declared himself against the possibility of a non-visual navigation system, maintaining that the bats in Spallanzani's experiments must have been damaged or disturbed. In Cuvier's opinion, a sense of touch in the body surface or wing membrane was the explanation of the bat's ability to avoid obstacles. At the time, this seemed a much more plausible explanation, and for another hundred years, the problem seemed to be solved.

Even when, in about 1900, two scientists were once again forced to the conclusion that bats are guided in flight by their sense of hearing, the idea that the phenomenon of nocturnal flight depended on sound was not able to gain general acceptance.

In 1920, Hartridge, a British physiologist, put forward the hypothesis that bats emit ultrasonic signals and receive back the echoes of these sounds. Just 18 years later, this fact was confirmed by the American zoologist Griffin working with the physicist Pierce. Pierce had constructed special apparatus that would detect ultrasonics. Insect interference to his studies prompted him to turn his attention to bioacoustics as a hobby. He had found that the shrill "singing" of insects is perceived only partially by the human ear, since it contains many frequencies that lie in the ultrasonic range. Griffin, who was working on bat migration, was interested in recording the shrill calls of bats as well. He obtained a few bats in 1938 and took them to Pierce to test Hartridge's theory. When the two workers placed the laboratory animals in front of the recording equipment, to their great delight, it registered sounds of great intensity, although to the human ear, the room seemed silent. They observed that when the noises were produced, the bat's mouth was always slightly open. So intrigued was Griffin by this result, that he began immediately to devote himself to a study of sound emission, echo detection and direction finding.

He refined the experiments and later, working with Galambos, established that closing the mouth of the bat led to disorientation. So it was clear: the transmission of sound is indeed by way of the mouth, while the larynx is responsible for creating the sound. Since then, it has become known that many species of bats fly with the mouth wide open, since it is in this way that the sound waves are projected. There are, however, a number of species that keep the mouth closed in flight, because in their case, the sound waves are sent out through the nose.

At almost the same time as Griffin, Pierce and Galambos, the zoologist Dijkgraaf working in Holland observed that even without the aid of electronic apparatus, but using only his extremely acute hearing, he was able to perceive the sound transmissions in bats as a quiet ticking like that of a wrist watch. He made the additional observation that the bat's sense of direction fails to function if the transmitter (mouth) or receiver (ear) is rendered nonfunctional.

So ultrasonic echolocation in bats was proved. Now it was known that obstacles are located by means of probe signals (ultrasonic sounds), the returning echo is received by the ears and thus perception of objects is made possible. The bats build up a sound picture of their environment. In the same way in which a landscape at night becomes visible to us as light thrown out by the headlights of a car is reflected from objects it strikes, so do bats recognize their surroundings hidden in darkness in the echo they receive from sounds they have emitted. They "see" by means of sound waves whether there is an obstacle in their flight path, requiring an alteration in the direction of flight. They "hear" the entrance to their sleeping quarters and the projecting ledge of rock on which they can roost.

After the Second World War, these findings were the prelude in a number of countries to a comprehensive programme of biophysical research into the further intricacies of this extraordinary sensory function in various species of bats.

Not every species transmits on the same frequency

Whereas the human ear perceives only sounds in the frequency range up to 20 kHz, that is, 20,000 cycles (oscillations) per second, the frequency range of the signals emitted by bats extends to 215 kHz. With an increasing number of oscillations per second, the length of the individual waves becomes shorter, and can be as little as 1.6 millimetres. And it is precisely the short waves that are best suited to produce usable echoes from small obstacles. They have the added advantage that they can be concentrated into a beam of sound. If the sound strikes a solid object, the energy density of the echoes bounced back can be quite high.

In order to analyze these sound waves, the scientist can display them on a cathode-ray oscillograph—equipment that depicts the oscillations in visual form on a screen. This will show that the signals made by the Vespertilionid bats that were tested are neither restricted to a single wave length, nor do they show a haphazard wave pattern. Rather are they in the form of a distinctive sequence of frequencies that in many species decreases sharply towards the end. For example, the frequency of the ultrasonic sound produced by the Little Brown bat (*Myotis lucifugus*), common in America, sweeps down from 100 kHz at the start of transmission to only 40 kHz at the end. Within one to two milliseconds, the call covers a frequency range three times as great as the total auditory range of the human ear. It may contain in all only about 50 sound waves, no two of which have the same wave length. If such a sound could be heard by man, it would not be a pure tone, but a chirp.

Many insectivorous bats of temperate and tropical regions belonging to the family of Vespertilionids that have since been investigated, produce this type of sound. This includes most of the European species of Vespertilionidae but not the Rhinolophidae. The emission of salvos of such chirps has led to the bats of this family sometimes being designated as "chirping bats". The frequency range in which the sounds lie varies between individual species, but always shows a drop of at least several kilohertz within the total duration of the sound. Minimum range of a sweep may be 15 or 10 kHz, but no Vespertilionid is known to call below 22 kHz, although some tropical bats are known much lower.

This characteristic modulation of the frequency range has earned another name for the bats that use this type of sound. They comprise the group of "frequency-modulating" or "FM" bats. But the "sound picture" mechanism is not the same in all bats. It soon became clear that diversity in the sphere of ultrasonic echolocation is greater than had at first been suspected. Other families were found to have quite different systems of echolocation, and many species use more than one system.

The Tübingen zoologist Möhres was the first to investigate the calls made by Horseshoe bats (Rhinolophidae), and found that these bats did not produce chirps but long-drawn, pure tones of up to 50 milliseconds duration with a short-frequency sweep at the end. As the bat takes wing or in cruising flight, the constant-frequency part of the pulses of sounds can reach a duration of 50 or even 100 milliseconds. In Möhres' opinion, these sounds are the purest of any produced by animals. They lie at a frequency which is characteristic of the particular species, although slight individual variations may occur. The Greater Horseshoe bat (*Rhinolophus ferrumequinum*) transmits at a frequency of 83 kHz, while the Lesser Horseshoe bat (*Rhinolophus hipposideros*) uses a frequency of 119 kHz.

Möhres made another very interesting discovery. He found that Horseshoe bats emit sounds through the nose, and as they do so, the complex nose leaf that earned the bats their vernacular name, serves to concentrate the high-frequency tones into a beam of sound that can be swept from side to side like a searchlight. The Rhinolophids can take bearings on their environment with great accuracy. What had seemed at first to be a useless ornament, a whim of nature, was suddenly shown to be an extremely practical, functional element in a sophisticated system of "auditory viewing".

The nasal excrescence carried by the family of Old World Leaf-nosed bats (Hipposideridae) has been found to fulfil the same function. Because of the different form of the nose leaf it does not focus the sound waves as sharply as that of the Rhinolophids. Analysis of the sounds showed a further variation in the Hipposiderids: the sound is in two parts. The first part is a very high, pure tone of 120 kHz. The final part corresponds to a chirp with a frequency range of 40 to 50 kHz. With this double system of acoustical location, the Rhinolophids and Hipposiderids are able to obtain information about nearby objects by means of the chirping part of the signal, and about objects considerably further away by means of the constant-frequency component.

In recent years, the zoologist Pye in Britain has examined the acoustical behaviour of representatives of many bat families. He established that both the frequency-modulating and the constant-frequency principles are met with in various families. Whether the sounds are emitted through the mouth or the nose does not affect the type of frequency pattern found. According to findings, certain representatives within individual families use the mouth as a transmitter, while other species in the same family emit sounds through the nose. Some groups have been found that use both mouth and nose as transmitter; for example the Long-eared bats *(Plecotus)*.

Measurement of distance by sound waves

In addition to the frequency and the ability to modulate it, another remarkable feature of many bats is the short duration of the ultrasonic sounds they emit. Within one millisecond, the sound waves travel 34 cm through the air. The echo from an obstacle at this distance returns to the bat's ear within two milliseconds. Since it is essential for the bat to hear the echo that returns from an obstacle or a quarry after its own emission of sound has ceased, these sounds must be of extremely short duration. It is quite possible for a chirp pulse to last for only 0.25 or at most 1 millisecond when an obstacle lies directly in front of the bat. The short, sound-free intervals are sufficient to prevent the sounds that are emitted and the echo that is returned from overlapping. Those species capable of frequency modulation judge the distance of an object by measuring the time delay between the outgoing sound and the returning echo. Information about the direction in which the reflecting object lies or in which an insect is flying is probably obtained from a comparison of the relative intensities of the echo reaching the right and the left ear. Of course, analysis of echoes received is not as simple as outlined here. In this sphere, there are many questions still unanswered today. One need consider only the

factor of time delay in echoes returning from objects at varying distances that would cause overlap.

The method of assessing range described here is problematical in the case of Horseshoe bats. Since in comparison with Vespertilionids, the tones they emit are of long duration, the echo returns while the sound is still being emitted. They have developed a different principle of echo reception. Their highly mobile ears move independently as they are turned towards the approaching echo and used as directional receivers. Depending upon the distance at which the obstacle lies, the echoes return with varying intensities, and from these differences in intensity, the Horseshoe bats are able to assess the distance to an object. In addition, an echo that an object reflects as it lies at an angle of 20° in front and to the left of the animal will have its maximum effect on the left ear, while its effect on the right ear will be less. These differences in intensity enable Horseshoe bats as well as Vespertilionids to assess the direction in which the obstacle lies. Anyone who is fortunate enough to observe a bat, particularly a Horseshoe bat, at rest before it takes flight, will be able to see from movements of the body, head and ears that for some considerable time beforehand, it emits ultrasonic sounds and thereby "examines" its environment.

Potentialities of ultrasonic echolocation

As bats fly into a cave, they emit 10 to 30 sound pulses per second. They have built up such an accurate sound picture of their day roost that they are familiar with every obstacle. Using their efficient place memory, they remember every detail, and so are able to move through their quarters without the aid of vision. It is estimated that, with their refined system of location, Horseshoe bats can perceive obstacles from a distance of 8 to 10 me-

Diagram showing oscillographs of ultrasonic echolocation pulses. Three sounds emitted by a Horseshoe bat (*Rhinolophus* sp.). These are pure tones of comparative long duration that can last up to 0.1 seconds. Frequency is remarkably constant diminishing only in the final 1.5 milliseconds (from Kulzer, 1957).

tres. Vespertilionids, with their bursts of sound, cannot rival this. They must come closer to an obstacle before reacting to it. If the bats are approaching a place at which they want to land, or if unexpected obstacles present themselves in their path, the emission of sound increases immediately to between 50 and 100 pulses per second. In this way, bats are able to continually gather up-to-date information about the unknown object.

Laboratory experiments have shown the amazing feats of which they are capable. A number of threads —decreasing in thickness in the course of these experiments—were hung close together across a space, to see when the bats would be unable to avoid contact with them. The first experiments carried out with Vespertilionids brought striking results. Not until they reached threads with a diameter of only 0.10 mm—the thickness of a human hair—did the bats touch them. Later experiments with Greater Horseshoe bats showed that this species even outshines Vespertilionids. They were still able to detect threads with a diameter of 0.05 mm.

This also explained why it had not been possible, until a few years ago, to catch free-flying bats in the nets used

to catch birds. The threads were much too thick. Experiments show that bats respond to threads of 3 mm thickness from a distance of 2 m, and threads of 0.18 mm from a distance of 1 m. So they still have sufficient time to turn aside. Only since the finest of nylon nets have been used, has it been possible to catch bats on the wing.

Analysis of the calls made by bats has shown, in addition to the findings mentioned above, that volume of sound is not uniform in all species. Particularly in those that catch flying insects or other animal prey, the ultrasonic sound is of high intensity. These bats screech through the night. Other species, for example fruit and nectar-feeders, produce much softer pulses, so that it is often difficult to record them. Since fruit-eating bats track down their food with the nose, these "whispering" tones are sufficient as a means of detecting obstacles.

The group of "whispering bats" consists of a wide variety of bats—including our Long-eared bats (*Plecotus* spp.) and the False Vampires (Megadermatidae)—producing a similar quality of sound for a wide variety of reasons. Vampires also belong to the group of "whispering bats". Because of their particular feeding habits, it is adequate if they can locate obstacles from a distance. So the sounds they produce are of low intensity. For Vampires, the senses of sight and smell are more important.

A series of sounds emitted by the Large Mouse-eared bat (*Myotis myotis*). The sounds begin with a sudden increase in pulse frequency and gradually die down. In 0.1 seconds, some 10 such sounds (chirps) are emitted. Duration of the individual sound is at most 0.005 seconds.

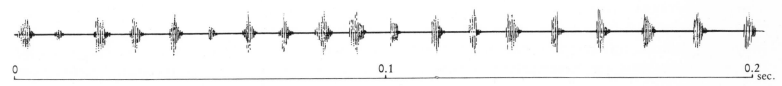

How do fish-eating bats locate their prey?

For a long time, the question of how or even whether fish-eating bats use their system of ultrasonic echolocation to catch their food was much discussed. It was known that the Fisherman bat *(Noctilio leporinus)* emits short sounds of high intensity through the mouth as it flies low above the surface of water. Observations of bats while they were fishing showed that this large bat does not rely on chance alone when it dips its hind feet with the sharp claws into water in order to catch a fish. Could it locate a fish swimming under water so accurately by means of sound waves? It is a fact of physics that only a small proportion of sound waves passing through the air will continue their path when they strike water. The surface of the water reflects almost the entire sound, and only about 0.1 per cent passes into the water. Similarly only 0.1 per cent of any echo would break out through the water/air interface. It is highly improbable that an echo from this faint sound bounced back from a fish would be perceived even by the sensitive organ of hearing of a bat.

Experiments carried out on bats in captivity finally solved the problem. Fisherman bats *(Noctilio leporinus)* were taught to take pieces of fish attached to the end of wires. When the wires were placed in a tank of water in such a way that the pieces of fish were entirely submerged, the bats were no longer able to locate their food beneath the surface. But when the surface of the water immediately above the bait was caused to move even slightly, the bat plunged its feet into the water and seized the prey. Clearly, *Noctilio* is not able to locate a completely submerged fish by means of ultrasonic echolocation, but is able to perceive the slightest of ripples in the water. So when a fish swimming beneath the surface causes waves on the surface, the fishing bat has no difficulty in locating the fish and seizing it.

Recognizing food by sound waves

The location of obstacles by echoes and the location and capture of insects are undoubtedly two skills of a different order. For years, scientists have been occupied with the problem of how bats are able to track down their prey at night. Spallanzani was one of the first to try to find an answer. His notebooks from the year 1794 tell how he blinded a number of bats and then released them. They returned to their roost in a bell tower in Pavia. Some days later, when he caught three of the test animals and examined the stomachs, he found that those of the blinded bats contained as many insects as those of normal bats. He was convinced that the bat's visual sense plays no part in the catching of insect food. But how could the insects be detected?

Later on, various scientists assumed that bats, with their acute hearing, are able to perceive the sounds made by insects in flight. But Griffin showed that this was unlikely. When he started to study the orientation sounds emitted by bats in the open country as well, he observed that bats catching insects intensified their succession of location calls, just as they did in manoeuvring to avoid obstacles. In experiments, the American Big Brown bat *(Eptesicus fuscus)*, a species closely related to the Serotine *(Eptesicus serotinus)*, was found to increase the rate of succession of its sounds as it flew towards prey from 10 to 150, even to 200 calls per second.

In the early sixties, after a good deal of preliminary work, Griffin and his colleagues were able to produce a laboratory analysis of the typical hunting behaviour of the Little Brown bat *(Myotis lucifugus)*. They released thousands of fruit flies *(Drosophila)* or mosquitoes *(Culex)*, and immediately the circling bats began to pursue them. From a distance of as much as one metre, the small insects were located and hunted with precision. The

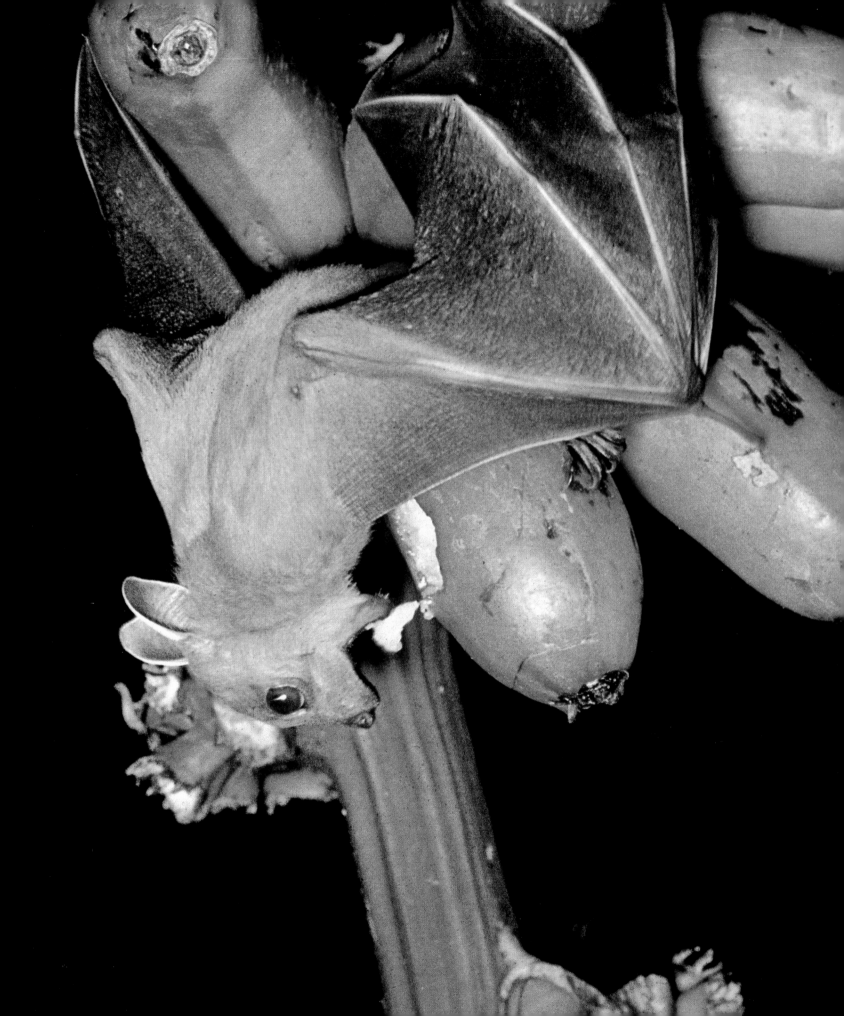

77 Pipistrelles *(Pipistrellus pipis-trellus)* eating mealworms. Even this small species of European bat can learn to eat its food from a dish.

78 A Little Brown bat *(Myotis lucifugus)* pursues a Tiger moth *(Apantesis virgo)*. With acrobatic flight manoeuvres, it uses its wings to try to force the prey into the tail membrane.

79 Two Fruit bats of the genus *Rousettus* in captivity, eating a banana.

80   Nectar bat (*Leptonycteris sanborni*; Phyllostomidae) visiting a cactus flower. To reach the nectar at the base of the flower, the bat must insert its head deep into the blossom.

81   The long tongue with bristle-like papillae at the tip is well adapted for feeding in this way.

82   When the bats leave the flower, the head is thickly coated with pollen. Part of it is licked off and eaten, with the rest the next flower is fertilized.

83   A Little Brown bat (*Myotis lucifugus*) catching a moth (*Arctia caja*)

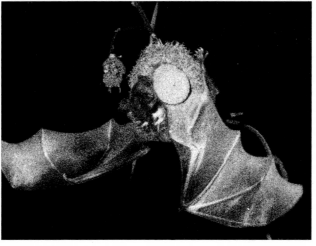

84 Pale Spear-nosed bat *(Phyllostomus discolor)* on a flower of *Hymenaea courbaril* (locust tree) in the Amazon region. The bat inclines its head over and down into the blossom, and licks up nectar in a second. The umbellated flowers are separated from the leaf shoots and so are easily accessible to bats.

85–87   The Pale Spear-nosed bat *(Phyllostomus discolor)* visiting a spadix of mimosa *Parkia auriculata* (Brazil), which consists of a large number of individual flowers. The blossoms extend beyond the foliage on long stems and so can be reached easily by the bats in flight.

The animals are scarcely able to gain a foothold on the flowers, so each visit lasts less than a second. Within this time, the bat licks nectar from the base of the fertile spadix while pollen from the blossom is transferred to its cheek, neck and chest.

88   Serotine *(Eptesicus serotinus)*. It is typical of the Vespertilionids that they emit ultrasonic waves through the open mouth in flight.

89   Brown Long-eared bat *(Plecotus auritus)* in flight. Among Vespertilionids, Long-eared bats are exceptions in that they can also emit sound waves through the nose. This bat is flying with the mouth closed.

135

90 Large Mouse-eared bat *(Myotis myotis)* in flight. Through its
open mouth, it sends out sound
waves into the night in order to locate obstacles and prey.

nearer the bat came to its prey, the greater was the rate at which the succession of sounds accelerated. At intervals of one or two seconds, and at the very moment when an insect was seized in an intricate flight manoeuvre, the cries reached a crescendo of sound which we hear as a "buzz" on a bat detector. In these experiments, it was also found that the bats are well able to distinguish between objects that are edible and those that are not. Apart from the insects mentioned above, mealworms, the larvae of meal beetles, were also thrown into the air. After about a week, the bats had learned to eat the mealworms. Now a number of plastic discs 3 mm in thickness and 16 mm in diameter were mixed with the mealworms which are about 2 cm long and 3 mm thick; and this "food mixture" was then tossed into the air. At first, the bats located both the mealworms and the plastic pellets, and rushed at the latter as if they were food. But within no more than a week, the first bats had learned to distinguish live food from simulated. 80 to 100 per cent of the mealworms were caught, while the plastic discs were rejected with a high degree of reliability (80-90 per cent). It is still not clear how the bats were able to distinguish one component from the other in the food supply.

The intricate and varied series of experiments illustrated definitively that bats locate and catch their insect prey by using echolocation.

This, of course, does not preclude the possibility that bats also perceive sounds made by insects. The zoologist Kolb in Bamberg produced some evidence for this. He was able to show that the Large Mouse-eared bat *(Myotis myotis)* could track down beetles that were not flying, but rustling among the floor litter of the test chamber.

The bat flew towards them accurately and then tracked them by nose.

Today, we are still a long way from being able to explain the entire phenomenon of ultrasonic echolocation. As each question is answered, the small creatures present new problems to the scientist. Bats are capable of performing feats that seem inexplicable to us.

The precision and accuracy with which the system of echolocation functions is of vital importance to them. Not only have they solved the problem of creating and emitting ultrasound, but also—and this is perhaps even more important—the problem of receiving back their own echo and distinguishing it from a multiplicity of competitive sounds. One can only marvel at the way in which even large numbers of bats flying about within an enclosed space seem not to disturb or confuse their fellows with their ultrasonic calls.

It is a remarkable achievement that the sense of hearing and the responsible brain centres are able to select a feeble echo out of the complex background of competitive noise made by other bats. Using two input channels, the ears, the brain can analyze accurately the direction of incoming noise and distinguish between the echo of its own location sounds and background noise that reaches the ear from other directions. It is not surprising that the acoustic centres of the bat's brain, which itself often measures no more than half a cubic centimetre, are highly developed and specialized. Research into the fine structure of these centres and into the functions of the brain that are the basis of the bat's amazing performances will continue to occupy scientists for many years to come.

Breeding habits

In previous chapters, so many peculiarities in the life of bats have already been described that it comes as no surprise to learn that the process of reproduction in bats also deviates from the general mammalian norm.

At about the turn of the century, scientists knew little about reproduction in bats. However, one of the first descriptions of parturition was given by the French naturalist Pierre Belon as early as 1555. Many of his observations accord well with accepted scientific findings of today. Until about twenty years ago, all that was known for certain about the reproductive biology of bats concerned various members of the family of Vespertilionid bats (Vespertilionidae) indigenous to Europe and North America and European Horseshoe bats (Rhinolophidae). But it is precisely these forms that show particularly great variation in their reproductive patterns. It was at one time assumed that the oestrus cycle in species of temperate latitudes did not begin until the spring, when they waken from hibernation. Only later was it discovered that most copulation occurs in autumn, although maturation of the egg does not take place at this time.

Since the habits of the many species are so varied, these findings could not be assumed to cover the reproductive biology of all Chiroptera. Recent research into tropical species in Africa, Asia and South America shows that there are many species-characteristic features of reproduction determined by geographical, primarily that is climatic, factors. For fruit bats in tropical regions, no separation in time has been recorded between insemination and fertilization. The deferment of fertilization until the spring in species living in temperate latitudes is a secondary adaptation to climatic conditions.

Findings on sexual behaviour, fertilization, period of gestation, birth and care of the young cannot be given general application. In many cases, information is available only on individual phases of the reproductive process. A good deal is known about the periods in which the bats assemble to give birth and rear young. In contrast, little is known of those times in which the bats disperse and live in isolation. Observation of tropical species of bats is rarely carried out continuously throughout an entire year, so that our knowledge of the reproductive biology of tropical bats is often fragmentary. Consequently, details described here apply only to selected representatives of individual families.

In temperate latitudes, the Microchiroptera do not possess secondary characteristics by means of which it is possible to distinguish the sexes. But in the tropics, in addition to those species that show no clear sexual dimorphism, there are some in which the males differ from the females by being larger and more intensely coloured. The nose leaf of the male of the Old World Leaf-nosed bat *Hipposideros larvatus* is said to differ in form from that of the female. In certain species, a localized, dense hair growth distinguishes male from female. The shoulder hair of the Epauletted Fruit bat *(Epomophorus)* has already been mentioned. In the Collared Fruit bat *(Myonycteris)*, the throat region has a dense covering of coarse hairs, and in various of the Tomb bats *(Taphozous)*, the males have such a distinctive "beard" that they can be recognized easily even at a distance.

Another sexual characteristic is especially important to bats in the breeding period, although it is barely detectable to the human senses. The bats have special skin glands that produce a strong-smelling, sexually stimulating secretion. In the mating season, these odorous substances are applied to the fur, wing membranes and even objects in the environment, in order to attract and stimulate sexual partners.

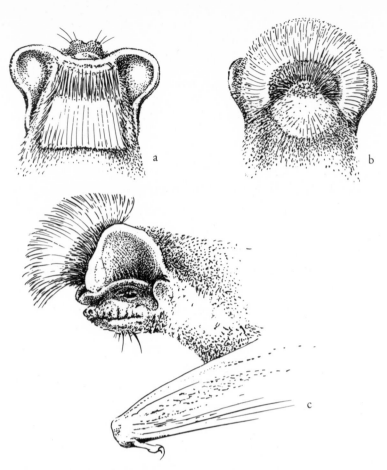

Adult male of the species *Chaerophon chapini* (Molossidae). An example of sexual dimorphism, a rare phenomenon in bats. Here, the male has a tuft of long hairs on the head (a) that stand erect during the phase of breeding (b, c) (after Allen, Lang and Chapin, from Brosset, 1966).

Factors affecting the reproductive cycle

In temperate latitudes, the reproductive process in bats, as in many other animals, is strongly affected by the annual seasonal cycle. In Europe, bats have only a few months during the summer in which to give birth to and rear their young. The food available between April and June must be used by the female to ensure the successful development of the embryo. An abundant supply of insects is vital in June and July to provide the mothers with enough nourishment to be able to feed the infant bats, while in August and September, the young bats that have become independent, as well as their parents, must consume a sufficient quantity of reserves to see them through six months of hibernation. The short summer of the Palaearctic and Nearctic regions provide just sufficient time to raise one litter.

The situation is more favourable for tropical species. They are not under such pressure in tending their young. Nevertheless, an annual rhythm of reproduction can also be observed in species living in regions with a very constant climate. The female again produces young only once each year. The birth occurs in the spring, or in the season that corresponds to our spring. This has produced an interesting finding. The same species that in the northern hemisphere gives birth in May/June, does so in the southern hemisphere in September/October. As the French zoologist Brosset discovered, the geographical equator does not coincide with the biological equator of bats. In Africa, a few degrees north of the equator, he observed species of *Rhinolophus* and *Hipposideros* with a typical seasonally-controlled rhythm of reproduction. But, like the populations south of the equator, they produced their offspring in September. Tomb bats *(Taphozous)* which in Bombay give birth to young in April, show a distinct delay in their reproductive cycle in Sri Lanka. Here, they do not bring their offspring into the world until September.

Particularly in the equatorial region, there are various species that are polyoestrus, they reproduce several times in a year. Among Microchiroptera, certain members of the Slit-faced bats *(Nycteris)*, Spear-nosed bats *(Artibeus, Glossophaga)*, Free-tailed bats *(Molossus)* and Sheath-tailed bats *(Taphozous)* have two mating seasons in the year. Most of these genera have two birth peaks: the first time in spring; a second birth follows towards the end of the summer.

Many species, Vampires for instance, show no recognizable annual rhythm. All year round, the colonies include pregnant and lactating females. In various species of fruit bats among the Rousette Fruit bats *(Rousettus)* and Short-nosed Fruit bats *(Cynopterus)*, the process of reproduction in many areas is not seasonal.

The important factor determining the frequency of parturition is undoubtedly the supply of food. Insectivorous or frugivorous species must produce their young when an optimal supply of food is available. For the sanguinivorous species, this is no longer important, they can find host animals all year round.

Since the majority of tropical species have a one-year reproductive cycle, the question arises of what are the factors that control the rhythm of reproduction in these species. It can scarcely be length of day, since close to the equator, day and night are of almost equal length. Nor do the seasons show such fluctuations in temperature and food supply as they do in northern latitudes. The rainy season might be a factor, but there is no evidence that this is the case. Clearly, this is a question still to be answered.

Sexual maturity and reproductive behaviour in bats

As far as is known today, European bats reach sexual maturity in their second year of life. Mating occurs first at about 14 months and the females are about two years of age when they produce their first young. But there are exceptions in this respect; *Rhinolophus ferrumequinum* reaches maturity mainly in its fourth year, whereas a few species, such as Pipistrelles *(Pipistrellus pipistrellus)*, have been found to give birth within their first year. Apparently only the female matures at such an early age; the male is not ready for mating until its second year.

Similarly, most fruit bats do not reproduce until their second year. Only the Rousette Fruit bat has been observed to copulate before it is mature.

Information on sexual behaviour and reproductive biology in bats in temperate regions has been obtained

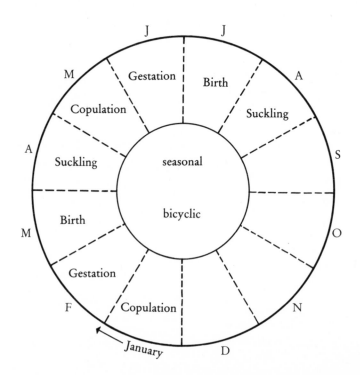

both by observing them in the field and studying them in captivity.

In Europe, when the young bats become independent in July or August, the maternity colonies gradually disintegrate. Old and young bats seek out different, temporary quarters before they make their way to the winter roosts. In these intermediate quarters, small groups consisting of males and females can be found. The sexual organs of the mature bats show that they are in a state in which fertile mating is possible. It is assumed that in many cases, pairing occurs there. Other indications suggest that the majority of females reach the winter roosts unmated, and that copulation occurs during the period of rest in the winter.

Mating in bats, in so far as it has been observed, is initiated by the male. In courting the female, the male makes use of acoustic as well as of olfactory and tactile stimuli. Since acoustic stimuli would have no effect on a sleeping female in winter quarters, it is probable that the sense of smell plays an important sexual role at this time.

Observation has shown that the selected female is awakened by bites on the neck, and when she has become active, copulation takes place. If the two sexes meet in their day-time roost, the male approaches the female and rubs his head against the side of the female's body. Usually this approach is accepted passively by the females, but those of certain species resist violently. Before copulation, the male of the Egyptian Fruit bat *(Rousettus aegyptiacus)* encloses the female in its wing membranes. The female objects to this strenuously and, shrieking, tries to escape. But usually, the male manages to seize hold of the female by an adroit bite on the back of the neck, and copulation can take place.

Tropical species mate at the day roost and only rarely outside it. The American Red bat *(Lasiurus borealis)* is alleged to copulate in flight. This seems unlikely.

Since bats are essentially promiscuous and apparently have no order of rank, it often happens that a single individual in breeding condition, male or female, may participate in acts of copulation with different partners several times in succession. Selection is entirely random and the partners probably never come into contact again.

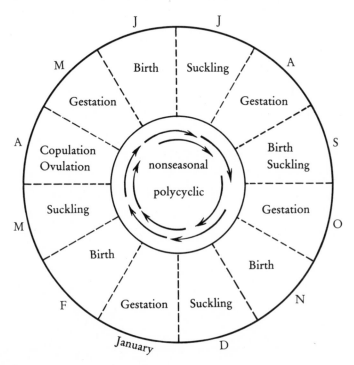

Reproductive cycles in various bats (in part after Wilson, 1973).
Seasonal, monocyclic reproduction in European bats. It is adapted to a food supply restricted to the summer half-year.
Seasonal, bicyclical reproduction in neotropical fruit-eating bats. No young are born in periods of reduced food supply.
Nonseasonal, polycyclical reproduction in Vampire bats. The individual stages of reproduction overlap and are not tied to particular months, since food is available to the bats all year round.

Problems of embryonic development in temperate latitudes

In those species that inhabit tropical regions, ripening of the sperm and ripening of the ovum are synchronized in such a way that fertilization takes place at insemination, and development of the embryo can begin at once. For bats of temperate regions, most of which mate in autumn, it would be unfavourable if embryonic development were to start immediately. The young would be born in the winter and would perish. So either fertilization does not occur at the time of copulation in autumn, or if it does, embryonic development is delayed or prolonged.

Either way, the result is that the offspring is not born until the early summer. Observation of indigenous species in captivity has shown that this involuntary delay in the process of reproduction is induced solely by the cold period of the winter months. If females that have been impregnated in autumn are kept in a warm room in winter and fed adequately, they remain awake and give birth to young much earlier than other members of their group living in the wild. That is, ripening of the ovum has started immediately and fertilization and normal embryonic development have followed.

These observations show that the sexual cycle in male and female does not normally progress synchronously. Whereas the male possesses fertile sperm from autumn until spring, it is only at the end of hibernation that ripening of the ovum in the female is initiated by means of a hormonal control mechanism. However, in most cases, insemination has already taken place months before this. The sperm must remain alive for five to seven months within the genital tract of the female, so that they can fertilize the egg in the spring. This is a phenomenon unique among mammals.

In spring, when the bats of temperate latitudes leave their winter roosts (hibernacula), the females group together and seek out their summer quarters, where they live in maternity colonies and give birth to their young. These quarters are familiar to the females; they return there year after year because the microclimate is a particularly favourable one. So strong are the bonds that attach the species to their summer quarters that they will even undertake long migrations from their winter quarters to their summer dwelling.

Maternity colonies—the "nests" of bats

Female Guano bats (*Tadarida brasiliensis*) cover distances of more than 1000 km in order to fly from Mexico to the southern states of the U.S.A., where they give birth to their young. Whereas in Europe, a maternity colony will consist of between a half-dozen and several hundred roosting females, the largest assembly of female Guano bats in the Eagle Creek Cave in Arizona at the beginning of the sixties was reported by American zoologists to comprise more than 20 million bats. The largest sea-bird colonies do not achieve concentrations on such a scale, and among terrestrial animals, they are found only in certain insects that live in social groups. The largest known "maternity colonies" of fruit bats are the mass assemblies found on trees at Cape York in Australia. It is estimated that four million bats rear their young there.

Observation of our indigenous species has shown that patterns of behaviour within the maternity colonies are very varied. On hot days, the colonies are loosely distributed, roosting under roofs or behind window shutters. When it is cool, the animals move closer together. The bats in a roost form a close community. But the nature of the bond that unites them is not clear. If they are constantly disturbed, the whole company makes off and settles in a different hanging area. In all, little is known of the behaviour in a maternity colony. It is, of course, very difficult to observe such large colonies in half-light and over a long period of time, particularly as they are in constant movement. In summer, the males are rarely to be found. They go their own way and take no interest in the fate of their progeny. The males of some species, such as the Parti-coloured bat *(Vespertilio murinus)* are also reported to live together in small colonies in the summer. In the Lesser Horseshoe bats, a number of males have also been observed living in the female maternity colonies.

In general, the number of young is limited to one. Twins occur rarely and multiple births have so far been observed only in a few species. The *Lasiurus* species of North America are recognized as particularly fecund. In their case, a litter may comprise two, three or four young.

This high number is not exceptional. The fact that the females each possess two pairs of nipples indicates how well they are adapted to a larger litter. Even in those species that bear only a single young, several egg cells (ova) are produced—in *Pipistrellus*, sometimes as many as seven. But it is not clear whether the remaining eggs are discharged unfertilized, or resorption of fertilized eggs takes place in the uterus. Only the embryo that is most favourably positioned within the uterus has the chance of further development.

The small number of offspring in bats represents an adaptation to flying. A gravid female carrying several embryos would be seriously impeded in its nocturnal feeding flight, which requires endurance and agility.

Various factors contribute to maintain bat numbers, in spite of the small number of young produced; for example, the considerable age to which bats can live, the long duration of reproductive capacity, and the small number of natural enemies. As to longevity, results obtained from bat banding have shown that the Greater Horseshoe bat *(Rhinolophus ferrumequinum)* can attain an age of 23 years, the Large Mouse-eared bat *(Myotis myotis)* 18 years and the Pipistrelle *(Pipistrellus pipistrellus)* 11 years. Large species of fruit bats have lived for more than 20 years in zoos. These maxima are only rarely attained. Average life expectancy is lower, standing perhaps at half these figures. Rats, mice and other rodents are known to live at most to only three to four years. Their numbers are threatened by many more enemies than are those of bats. It is not surprising that in order to maintain the species, rodents produce a higher number of young per litter and also more litters per year.

Environmental influences affect the period of gestation

For many species of bats of the Palaearctic and Nearctic regions, it is difficult to determine the duration of pregnancy, if impregnation occurred in autumn and it is not known at exactly what time in the spring fertilization took place. It is easier to determine the period of gestation for species of warmer regions, although here again, climatic factors can affect embryonic development. In comparison with other mammals that also give birth to young that are still considerably underdeveloped (nidicolous or altricial young), the long period of gestation in tropical fruit bats is surprising. It is five to six months for the large Flying Foxes, while smaller species give birth after four months.

Among the Microchiroptera, a gestation time of about three months has been estimated for small species of Old World Leaf-nosed bats (Hipposideridae) in India, but the Vampires of Central and South America do not give birth until after six to eight months. In cases where it has been possible to discover the period of gestation in species of temperate latitudes, it is found to be significantly shorter than for related species in hotter regions of the world. In temperate zones, a much extended pregnancy would be a disadvantage in biological terms, since the young must not only be born but also reared within the short summer months. Once independent, the young must make use of the late summer and autumn in order to achieve a peak of physical condition that will enable them to undertake the migratory flight to winter quarters and to overwinter there.

Small species *(Pipistrellus)* are pregnant for about 45 days and larger species *(Myotis)* for 50 to 65. But in temperate latitudes, climatic factors can cause great fluctuations in the period of gestation. If cold, wet weather in spring forces the female to reduce her activity and lower her metabolic rate, there is a delay in the development of the embryo. As a result, the period of pregnancy is extended. This environmentally induced retardation has been demonstrated experimentally. A moderate length of time spent in a warm room initiated the development of the embryo. After some time, a proportion of the animals were returned to cooler quarters (4 to 8 °C). They entered a state of hibernation and were examined three weeks later. It was found that in comparison with the animals that had continued to live in warm conditions, development of the embryos was distinctly retarded.

The phenomenon of delayed implantation, that is also found in other species of mammals, can be observed in the wild in those species of bats that lived originally only in warm areas, but which spread later into temperate latitudes. A typical example is the Long-winged bat *(Miniopterus schreibersi)*. In this species, the sexes have retained a synchronized reproductive cycle. When the female is mated in autumn, the ovum has already devel-

oped and fertilization is possible. But development of the embryo stops in the winter at the blastocyst stage, and the birth does not take place until early summer, that is, only when favourable conditions exist for rearing the young bat.

It is somewhat surprising to learn that this delayed embryonic development is also found in one tropical species. In the African Straw-coloured bat *(Eidolon helvum)*, fertilization takes place in early summer. Cleavage of the ovum, however, begins only in the rainy season in autumn. Thus, the embryo grows at the same time as the vegetation, and the young bat is born at a time of abundant food supply. Since embryonic development stagnates for about four months, and another four months pass before the birth, this species has a very long period of gestation of eight to nine months.

Links between mother and young

The process of birth and the position taken up by the female in labour differ among individual species. Most mothers do not give birth in the normal roosting position of hanging head downwards. In the maternity colonies, they have been observed to clamber up and away from the mass of bats, and to hang by the thumbs with head and body directed diagonally upwards. The young bat can emerge either head or hind quarters first, although breech deliveries are believed to predominate. During the birth, the female repeatedly attempts to assist the expulsion of the young, using the mouth or a hind leg. When the small, naked bat emerges, it does not fall into a warm nest, but in many species is caught in the tail membrane of the mother. The membrane is spread and curved into a pouch, and prevents the young bat from falling to the ground. As a result of their adaptation to life in the

92 Egyptian Fruit bat *(Rousettus aegyptiacus)*. These bats are about to copulate. The male has enclosed the female within its wings.

93 A pair of Egyptian Fruit bats with young, engaged in grooming.

94 Egyptian Fruit bat twins at the mother's breast

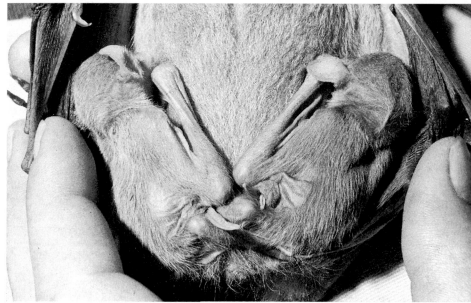

Egyptian Fruit bats *(Rousettus aegyptiacus)* with new-born young at the breast. The young bat has anchored itself so firmly to the fur of the mother that it cannot fall in flight.

96 Pipistrelles *(Pipistrellus pipis-trellus)*. Two seven-day-old young. Pelage has not yet developed; the wings have grown somewhat, but are not yet functional.

From the first day of life, the pointed claws of the large back feet allow the bats to gain a firm hold as they cling to the fur of the mother or when they are left hanging alone at night in the roost.

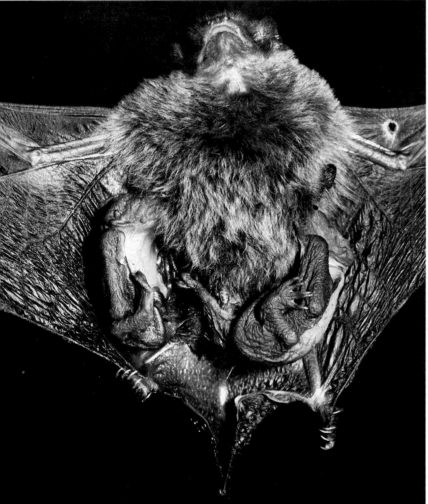

97 Pipistrelles *(Pipistrellus pipis-trellus)*. Female with new-born twins that have fastened themselves firmly to the breast.

98 Pipistrelle, three days old. The eyes are open, hair is scant, the wings still undeveloped.

148

99 Pipistrelles *(Pipistrellus pipistrellus)*. While the female consumes a mealworm, the young bat sucks milk from the mother.

100 Large Mouse-eared bats *(Myotis myotis)*. The young, about one week old, are still blind and almost hairless. They have been left at the roost while the mothers make their nocturnal flight in search of food.

101 Maternity colony of the Greater Horseshoe bat *(Rhinolophus ferrumequinum)*. The young are still incapable of flight. They have been left behind alone in the roof by the mother bats that are out catching insects.

102 Maternity colony of Large Mouse-eared bats (*Myotis myotis*) beneath a roof ridge. This large assembly consists mainly of young bats almost old enough to fly.

103   Angola Free-tailed bat *(Tadarida angolensis)*. Female with young on its back.

104   Angola Free-tailed bat. Young bat, a few days old, still naked. The clinging apparatus in the form of the large back-feet and the thumb are already well formed; the flight organ still incompletely developed.

air, bats have lost the ability to prepare a soft nest for their young. The mother herself provides a warm and protective refuge. The new-born bat crawls straight away into the fur of the belly and is covered by the wing membranes. Soon after the birth, it is hungry and seeks out the source of milk. It attaches itself to one of the two teats that are situated on the chest, and immediately begins to suck. Meanwhile, the mother licks the young clean and bites off the umbilical cord.

Although the period of gestation is long in comparison with that of many rodents, young bats at birth show a state of development that places them, together with mice and rabbits, in the category of nidicolous animals. In most species, the young are still hairless and blind, but already fairly large. Birth weight can be one fifth to one third of the weight of the mother. They are not yet able to fly, but crawl about in the parent's fur and maintain a firm hold with their relatively large feet and their thumb claws. Usually the mouth is attached firmly to a teat, providing a secure support.

Brood care is well developed in many fruit bats. For months, the instinct to hold fast to the mother is dominant in the young. In contrast to insectivorous bats, fruit bats take their young with them in the first few weeks on nocturnal flights in search of food. If the young bat moves too far away from the mother in the day roost, the latter calls it back again. Conversely, the young bat is able to communicate with the mother by characteristic sounds indicating that it is lost ("isolation calls"), whereupon the latter will begin to search for it. Since parent and young recognize one another by very specific scents, the bats in the large tree roosts always know their own.

The small bats attach themselves to the mother in a variety of ways, depending upon whether the mother's day roost is in the open or in a protected position inside a cave or building. Among fruit bats, they are often concealed beneath the protective wing membranes. In those species that do not hang freely from the branch of a tree or a roof, the baby bat finds a place of safety between the side of the belly and the surface against which the mother is hanging. In many of the Free-tailed bats, the mother carries its young on its back. Infant Horseshoe bats (Rhinolophidae) and Mouse-tailed bats (Rhinopomatidae) find special clinging aids on the body of the mother. She has two false teats in the pubic region which the young grip, attaching themselves by suction, during periods of rest.

Most species of bats show highly developed links between mother and young. Long-eared bats (*Plecotus*) or Pipistrelles (*Pipistrellus*) that have lost their young have frequently been observed to search for it intensively, and like fruit bats, they are able to locate it at quite considerable distances. Both acoustic and olfactory signals ensure recognition between parent and offspring. A new-born bat can already emit high-pitched sounds that lie just within the limit audible to the human ear. They are known as contact vocalizations or isolation calls.

For a long time, it was generally believed that in their first few days of life, young insectivorous bats were carried along with the mother at night. There are even photographs showing female bats in flight with their baby. But these pictures do not reflect the true situation. If, during the day, as the young bat clings to the mother, there is some sudden alarm, the female flies off with the young. But under normal conditions, the offspring is not taken on the nocturnal flights in search of food. From the very first evening, the new-born bats must remain behind alone. At this time, they cluster closely together and await the parent's return. Although they have, as yet, no system of heat regulation, they are not especially sensitive to low temperatures. When they are six days old, they are able to raise their metabolic rate spontaneously for the first time, but only when they have developed a full covering of fur are they capable of complete temperature control and able to adapt their body temperature to existing environmental conditions.

When the females return from their feeding flight, the piping calls of the young direct them back to their abandoned offspring. The mothers reply to these cries, land close to the young, crawl up to them and distinguish their own individual offspring by its scent and sound. The young immediately creeps to the mother and is provided with food, warmth and security.

In very large colonies of Vespertilionid and Free-tailed bats, the young bats hang together in flocks that are separated from the roosts of the mother bats. In the case of the Long-winged bat *(Miniopterus schreibersi)*, these flocks can comprise tens of thousands of young. In the American Guano bat *(Tadarida brasiliensis)*, there can even be millions of these small, naked, rosy bodies hanging close together in several large groups for mutual warmth. In face of such masses of young, the mothers are no longer able to seek out their own offspring. All accept shared responsibility for rearing this vast progeny.

When the female Guano bats return at dawn from their hunting flight, they land among the masses of hungry young. Those closest to them rush to this milk source to drink their fill. It hardly ever happens that a young bat fails to be fed, since two are able to be suckled by one female at one time, and the quantity of milk produced daily by the female can be as much as 16 per cent of her body weight. This is without precedent among mammals, as also is the manner in which the females care so selflessly for the well-being of the entire new generation, and behave with complete indifference to their own offspring.

This form of caring for the young can be compared only with the impersonal social organization in large insect communities, where care of the rising generation is also a collective task.

Apparently this is the only feasible way in which such vast nurseries can be organized and supplied. Of course, it has its disadvantages. For example, if a young bat that is still incapable of flight falls from the roof of the cave, it is doomed. There is no mother to respond to its cries, since none of them regards it as her own or is ready to show concern for it.

The development of the new-born and young bat

If the supply of food is abundant and regular, the small bats develop rapidly. Apparent disproportions in body form at birth, caused by the excessive size of the back legs and the undeveloped state of the wings, alter from day to

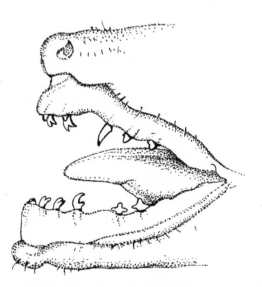

Deciduous teeth of a young Large Mouse-eared bat *(Myotis myotis)* at eight days old. The small, pointed milk teeth are hooked, enabling the young bat to attach itself firmly to the teats of the mother (after Eisentraut, from Natuschke, 1960).

154

day. The fore limbs grow rapidly and within six to eight weeks, the forearm has reached its adult length. Development is slower in the large Flying Foxes. They require almost a year to become fully grown.

Like humans, many mammals come into the world toothless. Nor do they have any need of teeth during the suckling period. But most species of bats deviate from this norm. The new-born bat already has well-developed dentition consisting of up to 22 milk teeth. These are known as "clutching teeth", since the hooked ends enable the baby bat to cling more readily to the mother. The milk teeth are shed in the first few weeks of life. There are also certain species such as Horseshoe bats (Rhinolophus) in which the milk teeth regress before birth, so no deciduous teeth are present. It is no coincidence that in these species, the mothers have "false teats" that can be gripped by the young with the mouth as an additional means of attachment.

In insectivorous bats, the various kinds of permanent teeth appear almost simultaneously, while in fruit bats, eruption of the molars may extend over several months.

Many of the details of development in the young, such as the opening of the eyes or the development of the pelage, depend on various ecological factors and differ slightly in almost every species.

Young Large Mouse-eared bats (Myotis myotis) have a clearly developed coat within four to five days of birth, while young Long-winged bats (Miniopterus schreibersi) still have only a slight hair covering after two weeks. The young of the Egyptian Fruit bat (Rousettus aegyptiacus) already have a fine covering of hair on the back at birth.

Many of the New World Fruit bats (Artibeus) have the eyes open from birth, young Mouse-eared bats can see when they are four to five days old, and young Pteropodid fruit bats do not open their eyes until seven to ten days after birth.

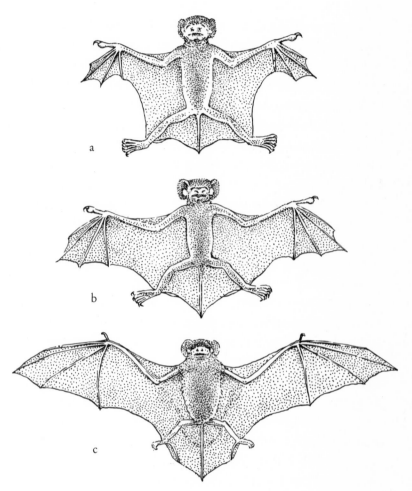

Alteration in body size-wing area ratio in the Common Noctule (Nyctalus noctula) in the course of development:
a 1 day old, b 28 days old, c adult (approx. 60 days old) (after Mohr, 1932).

With the development of the hair covering, links with the mother loosen, since temperature regulation is improving steadily. After two or three weeks, the young of many species roost on their own near to the mother, and go to her only to be suckled. The first attempts at flight are made at this time. It is important that the young do this in order to strengthen the muscles of flight.

155

In many species of the temperate latitudes, extremely high demands are made on the flight apparatus of young bats within only a few weeks of their becoming independent. Together with the older animals, they must undertake migratory flights to winter quarters, sometimes several hundreds of kilometres distant.

It is not altogether clear whether the mothers are able to satisfy the appetite of the young bats with milk alone until they are able to feed independently. Some reports suggest that the older bats frequently return to the young during the night to bring them supplementary insect food. This kind of mixed feeding is said to last for several weeks. But this seems very unlikely.

At the age of two months, the young are fully independent and must look for food themselves. The flight apparatus has completed its morphogenesis and is fully functional; it carries the creatures safely through the night. At first, flight is not as elegant and agile as it is in the adults, but the pattern of wing beats shows the character of typical bat flight. The growing bats do not have to learn from their parents how to fly. At a certain time they are simply able to fly.

The young of Vampire bats have the longest period of development among the Microchiroptera. They take nine months to become fully grown. For two months, they are fed only on milk, and then they must make the complicated readjustment to a diet of blood. At first, the mothers feed small quantities of blood by mouth, until at about six months, the young bats have developed sufficiently to be able to fly to the prey on their own. There is, however, no question of their being taught how to attack a victim and obtain blood. All the necessary behavioural patterns are innate in the animal.

Flight and self-sufficiency in feeding are possible only if the system of ultrasonic directional orientation is fully functional. Möhres was able to show that the isolation calls of the growing Vespertilionid bats gradually change over into typical orientation sounds. They are progressively diversified into an increasing number of pulses that become shorter and higher in frequency. During the first few nocturnal flights, orientation is not yet sufficiently perfected for the young to find their way alone. Möhres observed that they follow close "on the heels" of the mother, carried along in her sonic slipstream.

Comparative examinations of various species of bats have shown that the ability to emit sounds and the degree of differentiation in the first few days depends very much upon the stage of development of the new-born bat. If at birth the young are still very immature, without hair, with eyes and ears closed, their sound repertoire is restricted to faint cries of distress, the isolation calls, that are of somewhat extended duration. In those species in which the eyes and ears of the young are already open at birth, it is possible to distinguish several types of cry. But the frequencies are still lower than those of adult bats. Even quite soon after birth, the young of the Short-tailed Spear-nosed bats (Carollia) are able to emit the same frequency-modulated impulses as the parents.

Among large fruit bats, the growth and maternal care of the young extend over several months. Observation of the Indian Flying Fox (Pteropus giganteus) has shown the young still being suckled at five months and remaining with the mother until they are eight months old. Kulzer reports that the young of the Egyptian Fruit bat (Rousettus aegyptiacus) live in close association with the mother for four months. Long before that time, they are already capable of flight, and accompany the parents on nocturnal flights in search of food.

Development, which is rapid at first, later slows down and the young, although already self-sufficient, do not reach full body size until they are nine to twelve months old. In spite of the maternal care enjoyed by young bats of almost every species, not all grow to adulthood. Information on mortality in young bats is scarce and conflicting. Factors that can prove hazardous are very various. In many species, birth is a critical period, in others, the moment of separation from the mother.

In our latitudes, climatic factors more than any others threaten the life of the young bat. Cold, wet summer months, particularly at the time when the young are being suckled, can be disastrous for the new generation. If prolonged low temperatures prevent the mothers from flying for several days, or if they hunt for food in vain, the supply of milk decreases. As a result, the young are weakened and may even starve to death or be deserted.

Observations have shown that in summers with unfavourable weather conditions, mortality among the young in large maternity colonies of Mouse-eared bats is more than 40 per cent. The most important effect of bad weather is delayed births and weaning, making it impossible for the young bats to fatten up properly for the winter. Although there are no reliable data available, it is probable that excessively high temperatures also cause losses among young bats incapable of flight. And not least, man himself represents a threat to bats, particularly when he carries out measures of chemical conservation and insect pest control at the time when the young are being tended in the roosts.

Why some bats hibernate

The life of an animal depends very much upon the temperatures prevailing in its habitat. Only with optimal temperatures to which the animal is adapted will all bodily functions and behaviour patterns take their normal course.

In the earth's temperate zones, which include, for instance, Central and Northern Europe, the winter months with temperatures falling to below freezing point make special demands on the animal world. As a result, many species have adapted to these demands in such a way that they are able to survive the cold season of the year and avoid the danger of being frozen to death.

According to the manner in which the organisms adjust to the ambient temperature and alterations in it, they can be divided into cold-blooded animals or poikilotherms, warm-blooded animals or homoiotherms and as a subdivision of these, hibernating or aestivating animals or heterotherms.

The poikilothermic animals have a body temperature almost identical to that of the surroundings. They have limited ability to control the temperature of the body by metabolic processes, and therefore can tolerate extremes of temperature only with difficulty. In winter, unless they are able to find a place that is protected from frost, in which they can enter a state of torpor, they are unable to survive. These poikilotherms include not only the invertebrates but also certain vertebrates such as fish, amphibia and reptiles.

Only birds and mammals are able to maintain a constant body temperature. They constitute the group of homoiotherms. The ability to produce or dispose of heat as required makes it possible for them to hold the body temperature at the same level irrespective of changes in the ambient temperature.

If the temperature of the surroundings decreases, the animal must produce heat to maintain a constant body temperature. The production of heat presupposes a good supply of food. If food is scarce and there are no bodily reserves, the animals weaken, become cold and freeze to death.

Adaptations to the cold season

Most warm-blooded animals (homoiotherms) show a range of adaptations that help to prevent the winter months from becoming too great a burden for them. A change of pelage achieves better heat insulation, and reserves of fat laid down beneath the skin serve as energy stores. Many species of birds prefer to avoid the rigours of the cold weather and so leave these latitudes in autumn. They follow migratory routes to the south, where they survive the winter well in congenial temperatures and with a good supply of food.

For our bats, as well as for various rodents and insectivores, winter is a time in which not only the cold but also a shortage of food must be overcome. Certain species of bats, such as the Guano bat *(Tadarida brasiliensis)* are also known to undertake journeys in autumn, like migratory birds, in order to spend the winter in warmer regions.

But many of the species of temperate latitudes do not migrate in this way. They live through the cold season and the shortage of food by lowering the body temperature drastically, almost to freezing point. In doing so, metabolic processes are reduced so severely that the bats can survive the cold period without any intake of food, merely by using the energy reserves built up in the summer. In contrast to poikilothermic (cold-blooded) animals, they are capable at any time of active thermogenesis, that is, of waking from their sleeping state without an artificial input of heat. Mammals that employ this method are known as hibernating animals. Those of our indigenous European fauna include the hedgehog, the fat dormouse and the common dormouse, the souslik, marmot and hamster, as well as the bats. It is not long since bats were recognized as true hibernators. Some thirty years ago, they were still considered to be similar to cold-blooded animals. Nothing was known of the processes of temperature regulation and, contingent on them, the kind of safety measures bats have at their disposal to protect themselves from dying of cold.

Many hibernating animals bury themselves deep in the ground or build warm nests of grass and leaves. Not so our bats. They seek out caves or systems of galleries and cellars, and spend the winter there. Certain species live during the winter months in churches (e. g. the Pipistrelle, *Pipistrellus pipistrellus*) or hollow trees (e. g. the Common Noctule, *Nyctalus noctula*). Such quarters are suitable only if they fulfil two important conditions: they must be frost-free and humid. There are some species that can tolerate a few degrees of frost and are frequently found at the entrances to caves. Others prefer roosts with an air temperature of 5 or 10°C. High humidity is important since otherwise there is a danger of dehydration. For this reason, bats in their winter quarters are often found in places where the atmospheric humidity is so high that water vapour condenses on the bat's fur like pearls of dew when the surface temperature of the bat is less than that of the air. The method of temperature regulation employed during hibernation depends upon various metabolic processes and is slightly different in every hibernating species of mammal. With a considerable lowering of body temperature, bats enter a state of hibernatory torpor or lethargy. In summer months, a sudden fall in air temperature can induce a state of lethargy (torpor) during the day-time sleeping period. This phenomenon serves the same purpose as hibernation. Lowering the body temperature, even by only 10°C, reduces metabolism and conserves energy. The closer an animal brings its temperature to that of its surroundings, the less heat it loses externally. So it is not surprising to find that in the winter, body temperature can fall to 10°C, 5°C or less, depending upon the ambient temperature.

In a state of lethargy, the bats hang with no sign of life on the walls and roof of their roosts. Externally, this state resembles the torpor induced by cold in poikilotherms. However, the two quiescent states cannot be equated. Since poikilotherms possess no means of thermoregulation, they must necessarily go through all the fluctuations in temperature of the environment. Bumble-bees, frogs and lizards warm up and cool down passively. In the first few days of life, young bats still react like poikilotherms or cold-blooded animals. Their regulatory system must first develop before they can actively raise their temperature by increasing metabolism. The existence of a regulatory device of this kind permits hibernating bats to survive at low temperatures, and to emerge from this state actively, by developing the higher body temperature, even though the ambient temperature remains low. Bats then, in contrast to cold-blooded or poikilothermic animals, are not entirely dependent on the environment for the level of their body temperature.

The period of hibernation starts in October/November and ends in March/April. The species most sensitive to cold appear in the roosts first and usually sleep for the longest period. Some cold-resistant species, such as the Pipistrelle, can still be seen flying about in the open in December. The last bats disappear with the arrival of prolonged frost, when the regular supply of insect food is insufficient.

Year after year, the bats return to the same roosting quarters, where they enter a state of lethargy, hanging in large clusters (e. g. Large Mouse-eared bats), in small groups (e. g. Daubenton's bat and the Pond bat) or individually (e. g. Long-eared bats, Lesser Horseshoe bats), with the hind feet hooked to the roof, walls or into crevices. Those species that insinuate themselves into cracks and niches in the deepest recesses of caves live in a microclimate that is virtually unaffected by fluctuations of temperature in the surroundings.

Most species show distinct preferences in the temperature of their roosts. Since they are capable of registering temperature fluctuations of less than 1°C, they will sometimes move to a different hanging place within the roosting area, if there is a change in temperature. On the other hand, a single species has a different preferred temperature for different months of the winter and young bats may select different temperatures from adults. The reasons for this are not clear, but are probably related to the decreasing amount of stored energy. In the winter roosts, several species are frequently found together.

A visit to such a roost is always an impressive experience. Seeing the creatures hanging there, it is difficult to believe that there is any life at all in the small bodies. The eyes are closed, the body cold to the touch and incapable of coordinated movement. In their hibernatory sleep, the bats are utterly vulnerable to any enemy. Fortunately, apart from man, they have few enemies.

Hibernation in mammals is not a prolonged sleep lasting for six or seven months, for the animals waken spontaneously at intervals of several days or weeks. In many of the hibernating animals, waking phases last hours or even days. The pattern of sleep varies greatly between species. For bats living in simulated winter conditions in the laboratory, sleep periods of up to 30 to 80 days have been recorded. This is considerably longer than the period of continuous sleep recorded for other hibernatory mammals. Many winter sleepers use these interruptions in sleep for the excretion of urine and faeces. Many bats use warm winter spells to feed up and drink. There are good numbers of flying insects available from time to time during the winter. Bats of northern latitudes, often use the hours of waking to alter their hanging place or even to move to different quarters if the old ones have become cold or draughty or too warm. Mating may take place during these phases.

What signals the bats' departure for the winter roost?

What is it that tells bats that the time has come to make for winter quarters? Just as the alternation of light and dark establishes the diurnal rhythm of animals, so it is clear that light also affects their seasonal rhythm. In addition, other "signals" from the environment announce the approach of winter, such as the sudden onset of cold weather in the autumn, or a perceptible decrease in the supply of food. A characteristic adaptation to severe fluctuations in temperature that can be observed in bats even in summer, is that during a prolonged cold spell in autumn, the bats no longer waken every night, but extend the day-time period of lethargy over several nights.

All these "key stimuli", as they are called by the behaviourist, together with a certain instinctive hibernatory urge, prompt the bats to set off on one particular day on their flight towards winter quarters.

Once they have reached the accustomed roosts, a few days of adaptation to constantly low ambient temperatures of between 3°C and 8°C induces a state of lethargy in the bats. The speed at which the body cools, in spite of being under the control of the brain, depends primarily upon the temperature of the surroundings. The greater the difference between skin temperature and external temperature, the more rapidly does cooling proceed. Since there is a lower limit of temperature for developing the state of lethargy, the bats first "test" whether they are able to achieve this state or not in the place that they have selected as a roost. If it is too cold at the chosen site, there is a danger that the bats may not succeed in raising the level of heat production, and may die of cold.

Lowering of the body temperature and, with it, a gradual deceleration of all physical functions, is brought to a halt at an intermediate point. By increasing the cardiac rate and respiration, the bat manages to reawaken. Once again, there is a reduction of temperature, this time to somewhat lower levels, and the process of waking is again "practised". Finally the bats reach the level of hibernatory temperature at which they hang for days or weeks at a time.

For many tropical species that are able to enter a state of lethargy during their day-time sleep, the lower threshold temperature is still relatively high. They are able to waken from a state of lethargy only if the ambient temperature remains above a critical level. If it falls below it, active re-warming is no longer possible. In Vampires (Desmodus), the minimal level is 20°C and in Lesser Tube-nosed Fruit bats (Nyctimene), as high as 25 °C. Members of the family of Old World Leaf-nosed bats (Hipposideridae) living in the tropics also show only slight tolerance to persistent cold.

For the hibernating bats of our own latitudes, the ambient temperature can fall a good deal further. It has been found that it can be dangerously low without the animals waking. They are assured of active re-warming because the "thermo-regulator" within the animal can maintain the body temperature at a particular minimum—the lethargy level. Bats in hollow trees have been observed to continue sleeping even at air temperatures of −5°C to −8°C, and to adjust their minimum temperature. One very frost-resistant species is the American Red bat (Lasiurus borealis). It spends the winter outdoors on the branches of trees. Sometimes it has even been snowed under at temperatures below freezing point. To keep the body temperature above 0°C and to avoid heat loss, these bats bring the large hair-covered tail membrane up to completely cover the lower surface of the body.

The lowest recorded body temperatures during hibernation vary between 1°C and 5°C according to species. If the temperature falls below this, some supercooling occurs, but if it falls below freezing point, the bats freeze to death. But this stage is rarely reached. Very low temperatures have the effect of an alarm signal. The cardiac rate rises, the bats wake up and look for a more favourable roost.

Vital functions proceed "at the economy rate"

It is interesting to consider the changes that take place in the animal as a result of intense cooling, when all vital processes are reduced to a minimum. A drastically restricted provision of energy of this kind heats the body only just sufficiently to prevent death. The chemical processes in the cells of a homoiothermic (warm-blooded) organism are very well adapted to low temperatures. Yet very little is known in detail about them, even though this particular phenomenon could have extremely important human applications.

Retardation of circulation during hibernation can best be detected in the engine responsible for circulation, the heart. Whereas the heart of a hibernating animal continues to beat at temperatures of around freezing point, any cooling of a fully homoiothermic animal to temperatures of between 10 and 20°C has a critical effect on circulation and proves fatal. In hibernating bats that are sleeping deeply, the heart-beat is scarcely perceptible. Cardiac rate is drastically reduced. The heart of a Large Mouse-eared bat *(Myotis myotis)* that beats 400 times a minute when the bat is awake, and 800 times when in a state of excitement, now falls to only 15 to 20 beats a minute. It is not really possible to specify an exact cardiac rate since this feature is influenced by many factors and shows frequent spontaneous increases. Since with such a low pulse rate, blood flow is only slight and moreover, the blood vessels are greatly constricted, the "superfluous" blood is stored in the major veins of the body.

Not only does the heart beat more slowly than when the bat is awake, but respiration is also much reduced. Several seconds may elapse before an observer sees a hibernating bat draw breath at all. Sometimes there is a periodic grouping of breaths, in which series of breaths are drawn in and expelled, with intervals of several minutes between the groups.

If a bat is disturbed, regular breathing begins immediately. This shows that in deep hibernation, respiration, like circulation, is still under the control of the brain. The greater part of the stored reserves of fat are required for the activities of arousal, and so only a little is available for the actual process of metabolism. If bats had to remain awake throughout the winter in an ambient temperature of about 5°C, they would have to produce one hundred times the amount of heat. But there is not sufficient food available for this, so restriction of the energy expenditure is the only way to survive the cold season.

Because of the extremely low metabolism, waste products are few. The quantity of urine in particular is only 1 per cent of its level during the active season. This is a considerable advantage to bats, since otherwise important mineral salts would be lost from the body.

It has frequently been suggested that the state of lethargy is a primitive characteristic and indicates a certain inadequacy in the heat balance of hibernators. While it is quite true that their heat balance is organized differently from that of non-hibernating animals, they cannot, for this reason alone, be considered as primitive or underdeveloped. On the contrary, this specialization in heat regulation which allows bats to reduce the expenditure of energy during every period of sleep and enables all hibernators to survive the cold season of the year, is a functionally expedient adaptation to extreme living conditions.

By actively increasing the rate of heart-beat and respiration and at the same time, dilating the blood vessels, they are capable of re-warming the body at any time. The warming process is initiated in two ways: on the one hand, violent shivering produces heat, and on the other, the body temperature is raised in a special, "non-shivering" manner. The first form, known as shivering thermogenesis, is a familiar process. It is one we can observe in our own bodies, when, after remaining too long in cold water, rapid contractions of the muscles cause shivering and our teeth "chatter with cold". This action of the muscles increases metabolism enormously and is an important source of heat.

"Non-shivering" heat is also produced partly from the musculature but to a much greater extent from the tissue known as "brown fat". By eating extra food in autumn, bats, like other hibernators, build up a reserve of this fat, storing it between the scapulae and along the spine. The significance of the brown fat tissue was unclear for a long time, although it was given the name of the "hibernating gland". Today, it is known that it represents the bat's energy store, allowing for intensive chemical production of heat. The supply of fat is used slowly both to maintain vital functions at the much reduced "economy rate", and to allow spontaneous arousal from hibernation at fairly frequent intervals. From the loss of weight during the winter months, it is clear how large is the proportion of fat reserves that bats accumulate in autumn as winter provisions. Examination of various species shows a weight loss in spring, compared with the creature's weight in autumn, of 25 to 35 per cent. It is particularly important for the females to enter hibernation in autumn with energy stocks as large as possible, since in spring, these reserves must also ensure the start of embryonic development.

Brown fat occurs in non-hibernating mammals, including man, only for a short period after birth. As soon as the ability to raise body temperature by shivering has developed, this tissue loses its thermo-regulatory significance and regresses. It is clearly a primitive characteristic of mammals, which in its further development in hibernating animals became a factor of vital importance to them.

No oversleeping in the spring

It is surprising how bats waken from their winter sleep and emerge from their dark winter quarters at exactly the time when the cold season is past and new food supplies are available. What timing mechanism arouses them at the right time? The so-called "biological clock" that controls the innate circadian rhythm of activity in animals undoubtedly also has a certain effect on hibernation, but cannot bring it to an end.

Since the internal rhythm frequently deviates from a strict 24-hour periodicity, and during the winter months the bats do not waken for days or weeks at a time, the synchronization between the day's course and the biological clock must be lost in hibernation.

In those bats that roost near the entrance to the cave, the rise in temperatures outside in the spring undoubtedly plays a part as an arousal stimulus. But this cannot affect the many species that roost in the farthest depths of caves where temperature is constant. There must exist some other arousal mechanism within the animal itself.

One can assume that during the winter months, internal histological changes occur within the organism as a result of increases in the products of metabolism, so that the bat would die, if it did not waken at a particular time and restore balance in its inner processes. These changes apparently affect the relevant centres of the brain which bring about the restoration of normal body temperature, and thus cause arousal of the animal. It is also possible that these brain centres are stimulated by way of certain sense organs and then begin to function. In either case, arousal would be triggered off as a reflex.

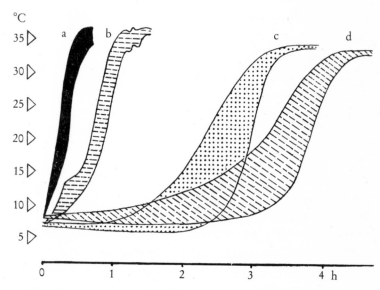

The pattern of temperature increase in various mammals on arousal from hibernation
a bat   b garden dormouse   c golden hamster   d common hamster (after Raths, modified, 1977)

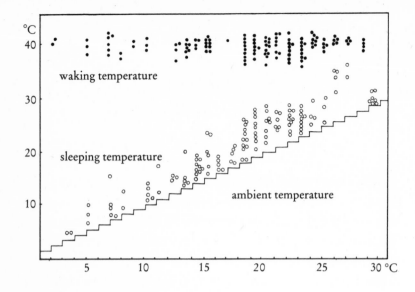

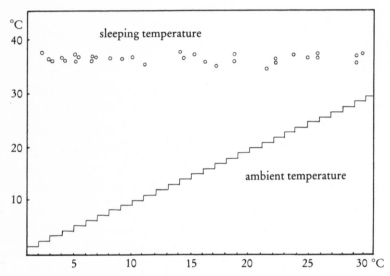

Sleeping and waking temperature correlated to ambient temperature in:
a Large Mouse-eared bat *(Myotis myotis)*. Sleeping temperature is only
a few degrees above ambient temperature.
b Indian Flying Fox *(Pteropus giganteus)*. In fruit bats, body temperature
is kept constant during sleep. It is entirely independent of the ambient
temperature (after Kulzer, 1965).

But here one should not overlook the fact that at such
low body temperatures, various of the animal's sense organs respond to stimuli only minimally or not at all. At
temperatures of below 12°C, hearing in bats is reduced,
and at less than 5°C, bats are effectively deaf. In hibernating hamsters, the retina of the eye is insensitive to stimuli. But the nerve tissue has not entirely lost its ability
to function, since even in hibernation, bats are capable of

many reflex actions. If these apparently lifeless creatures
are lifted from their hanging place, the legs perform
searching movements and when the toes have found a
support, they hook on to it firmly by reflex action. The
sensory cells of the skin which react to pressure, temperature and pain are not entirely blocked by cold. So it is
not impossible that the cutaneous receptors become so
highly sensitive as a result of the altered internal condition of the animal that they give off spontaneous arousal
stimuli.

When bats waken, it is essential that they warm up rapidly. The lower the ambient temperature and therefore
also the body temperature, the slower is the process of
arousal. Their relatively small body size is an advantage,
since smaller animals warm themselves more rapidly
than large ones. It has been found that the body temperature rises by 0.5°C to 1°C per minute, that is, with an
ambient temperature of 5°C, the bats have attained their
normal waking temperature of 38°C after approximately
an hour.

It is interesting that the front part of the body warms
much more quickly than the hind quarters. This is not
mere chance. It means that the body mass which is heated
initially is small, and that in particular, the vital centres of
the head and chest region are enabled to function normally as quickly as possible.

Arousal requires a high expenditure of energy, yet the
stored reserves of fat must be sufficient for the long period of hibernation. As a result of repeated spontaneous
awakenings throughout the winter, it is estimated that
under normal conditions, two thirds of the stored energy
is consumed.

However, if the animals are disturbed frequently in
winter, their energy reserves drop to critical levels. Since
bats in hibernation react to every change in temperature
and to every stimulus of touch and light by waking, it is

essential that disturbance of winter roosts should be avoided.

Once the temperature of the head region has been raised to 15°C by heat produced from the brown fat, the muscles begin to shiver and help to raise the body temperature further. In addition, other stored energy reserves such as sugar, glycogen and even the body's own proteins are mobilized in order to advance the increase in temperature.

Since all processes of metabolic combustion are associated with a high consumption of oxygen, the bats can be seen to breathe heavily on arousal. Once the waking temperature is reached, normal body movements begin. The environment is examined by the bat's system of echolocation, a great quantity of urine is given off and extensive grooming begins. But the bats do not remain for long in the place that has sheltered them through the winter months. It is time to seek food and replenish the much depleted energy stocks. The bats fly out from caves and crevices in walls, rest initially in intermediate roosts before setting off on longer or shorter migration flights, to arrive in April, May or June in their maternity colonies.

It is still not clear how bats evolved this complicated thermo-regulatory system which makes it possible for them to hibernate and to enter a day-time state of torpor.

In the course of evolution, there was an initial segregation of bats into those species which always show a constant body temperature and those in which the body temperature adapts itself to that of the surroundings. All fruit bats belong to the first group; they are good homoiotherms. On the other hand, certain species in the families of Vespertilionid and Horseshoe bats can lower their temperature to almost 0°C. This has enabled those bats to adapt to the cold season in our latitudes.

Between these two extremes, there are various species that represent intermediate stages in thermoregulation. For example, Free-tailed bats can reduce their temperature to only about 20°C. If it falls below this, they are not able to warm up again. Although these species can enter a reversible state of heterothermia daily, they are not capable of true hibernation. So they are unable to spread further northwards. Individual representatives of this family have extended their territory as far as the south of Europe and of North America.

Species belonging to the families mentioned above (Vespertilionid and Horseshoe bats) that live in the tropics can lower their body temperature to that of their surroundings when they sleep. This decrease is much slighter than it is in our indigenous species, since the air temperature in the day roosts of many tropical Microchiroptera is often only a few degrees below the external temperature. But if the ambient temperature happens to drop too far, the tropical species react differently from those of the temperate regions. They do not become torpid but enter a state of alarm instead. All physical functions are intensified, heat is produced and the bats remain awake.

Since the supply of food in the tropics does not fall to such a low level as it does here in the winter months, it is unlikely that heat regulation will be threatened. However, in experiments, the Tübingen physiologist Kulzer was able to induce hibernation for a period of three weeks in Mouse-eared bats from tropical Australia. In that time, the creatures showed the same metabolic changes with which we are familiar in our own hibernating species.

These results indicate that the capacity for heterothermia is a character of bats which evolved even before they began to spread out across all the continents of the world.

1000 kilometres without a compass

It is well known that many mammals undertake regular seasonal migrations along routes which vary greatly in length. Among these migratory mammals there are various species of bats. Their capacity for flight is a considerable advantage, allowing them to cover long distances in a very short time.

Observers long ago noticed that some species of bats are to be seen during winter in areas in which they occur only in small numbers or not at all during the summer. From this they concluded that the species living in mountainous regions move to the lowlands in winter and species that extend almost as far as the polar circle make long migrations in autumn to regions further south. Because bats lead a very secretive life and restrict their activities largely to the hours of darkness, much still remains to be discovered about bat migrations.

Lack of food and cold weather compel a change of abode

There are various factors that can induce bats to move a longer or shorter distance to a new home. In the tropics, migration has been observed principally among large fruit-eating bats, the Megachiroptera. They leave their roosts at particular times of the year when food becomes scarce and move to areas in which it is plentiful. The Grey-headed Flying Fox (*Pteropus poliocephalus*) of Australia is reported to migrate in spring (October) from Queensland southwards along the east coast to New South Wales to reach the Sydney area in the middle of November. Huge flocks of the bats cover more than a thousand kilometres in the course of a few weeks. They arrive in the south at exactly the time when the wild figs and the many succulent fruits ripen in the large fruit plantations. Here they are assured an abundant supply of food. Even so, it is not certain that all the bats of the northern regions take part in these long migrations to the south.

Migratory flights that are closely linked to the time at which fruit ripens are also known to take place among African species of fruit bats. Wahlberg's Epauletted Fruit bat (*Epomophorus wahlbergi*) appears in South Africa at just the right time to help itself to the fruits ready waiting there. In the Congo, migrating Straw-coloured bats (*Eidolon helvum*) have been observed on their way to new feeding grounds.

Another reason given for movements on a large scale in tropical and subtropical species, in addition to a shortage of food, is the excessive heat of the summer months. Since the temperatures in certain zones reach intolerable levels, the only course of action open to bats is to fly into regions of more agreeable climate.

No individual studies exist on migratory behaviour, routes, direction of travel and distances covered by tropical bats, particularly Flying Foxes. So far, detailed research on these subjects has scarcely been possible, since the practice of marking bats by means of wing clips, much used in studying the bats of temperate regions, has rarely been applied to tropical populations. So far, information about the migrations of tropical bats has come largely from chance observations.

Reliable information on the migrations of bats exists in particular for the species of the Palaearctic and Nearctic region. In these areas, it is the cold season and the inadequacy of food which cause the bats to leave their summer quarters.

Among the species of the temperate latitudes that are unable to hibernate are the Guano bats (*Tadarida brasiliensis*), of which the females leave the summer roosts in the caves of Texas and New Mexico, U.S.A., in autumn after the young have become self-sufficient, to migrate southwards over distances of up to 1000 kilometres to Mexico, where they spend the winter. Observations have shown that they cover this migratory route very rapidly, for in no more than three weeks, the first Guano bats have reached their winter roost. Here, it is warm and food is plentiful. With the arrival of spring, millions of these bats set off once again on their migratory flight northwards to the maternity colonies. It has been found that most of the males of this species remain in Mexico and await the return of the females in the autumn. But it is clear that a good many females also elect not to join in the great migration, but give birth to their young in the winter roost. Why should this be? So far, no one has discovered what factors determine which of the bats fly off and which remain.

Most species of the temperate regions hibernate, and move from their summer quarters into frost-free caves, tunnels or buildings. The distance covered may be only a few kilometres, but occasionally can be more than a thousand.

Three North American species, the Red bat (*Lasiurus borealis*), the Hoary bat (*Lasiurus cinereus*) and the Silver-haired bat (*Lasionycteris noctivagans*) are known to migrate over long distances. They spend the summer in the north-east of the United States and in Canada. Here they show themselves to be particularly resistant to the inclemencies of the weather, since they hang during the day almost entirely without protection among foliage or against the trunks of trees. If the weather becomes too disagreeable, they leave their summer home and begin to migrate southwards in small troupes. From the end of August until November, representatives of these species are found in regions along the Atlantic seaboard of America where they are scarcely ever observed in summer. The females in particular travel as far as the southern states of Georgia and Florida. Here the winter

months are so mild that they hibernate for only a short period. On their migratory flight along the Atlantic coast, these species of bats perform amazing feats of flying. There is no obstacle that can halt them as they cover this great distance. They cross ocean inlets in continuous flight. Seafarers have reported seeing these species far out at sea, where they sometimes land on the rigging of ships in order to rest, or else fall there from exhaustion. They have been found in autumn and spring on barren islands out in the ocean from which they are absent at other seasons of the year.

These observations indicate how it is possible for members of the *Lasiurus* species to reach even the Bermuda Islands that lie some 1200 km from the mainland.

The seasonal migrations of the three North American species of bats described here are probably those which approximate most closely to the migrations of birds. In most cases, the biological significance of migration is different for bats of the temperate regions than for migratory birds. At the beginning of the cold season, our bats leave their summer quarters to seek out frost-free winter sleeping places. Birds, on the other hand, move to the warmer south where they escape from the cold of winter, and where an adequate food supply makes it possible for them to continue their life in its normal way.

It is not possible for bats to inhabit the frost-free retreats throughout the whole of the year. In the summer, it is too cold in the caves and cellars: the bats would be in a continual state of torpor. So at the start of the warm season, they are obliged to move into summer quarters. Only the males of various species are still to be found in summer in rock crevices, cracks in walls and beneath bridges. They require less heat, indeed cooler temperatures are more favourable for spermatogenesis. Consequently they sometimes use the same roost throughout the winter and summer.

Bat banding with wing clips aids scientific research

In order to obtain more information on the migration of bats, it was necessary to mark the bats. The practice of marking birds by means of leg rings in order to discover their migration routes had already been introduced by ornithologists and had obtained remarkable results.

So in 1932, Eisentraut, the great authority on bat research, began bat banding in Germany. The method had first been employed in 1916 by the American zoologist Allen. He used bird rings, attaching them to the hind legs of the bats. Bat banding in the U.S.A. took on a much increased impetus in the thirties. From 1939 onwards, the rings were attached to the forearm, since the small hind legs are less suitable for the attachment of rings.

Right from the start of his planned programme of banding, Eisentraut used specially designed flanged aluminium "rings", or they might better be described as wing clips, which were fitted around the forearm. With a band of this kind, the bat carries an identification tag, usually for the rest of its life; whenever it is caught or wherever it flies, it can be identified at any time. In Germany, bat banding groups expanded rapidly and bat researchers in other European countries also adopted the method with enthusiasm. In 1932 Ryberg in Sweden, in 1936 Bels in the Netherlands, and in 1937 members of the Soviet Academy of Sciences in the U.S.S.R. took up the banding of bats. Many European countries as well as Australia, Canada and Mexico followed their lead, and a well-organized system of banding has been established. In contrast, it must be said that the use of bat banding for scientific research has scarcely been developed at all so far in the tropical regions of Africa, Asia and South America which, of course, are the principle territories of the bats.

In order to coordinate the increasing activities of marking, most countries have set up a central office of banding. These central offices organize the manufacture of the bands and their distribution to interested colleagues. Each band is stamped with an individual number and an abbreviated address so that it can be returned by the finder to the correct office.

In addition to this method of banding which is widely used today, other methods of marking bats have been tried out by various workers. For example, marked tags have been attached to the ears, or a coded pattern of perforations have been impressed or tattooed on the wing membrane. The ear tags have the advantage that they cannot be damaged by the teeth of the bat, but it is possible that they hinder to a considerable extent the reception of ultrasonic sound waves. Tattoo marks and perforations fade or knit together and so are good, but only for short-term studies.

It must be said that even the bands have certain disadvantages. To the bat, the band is a disagreeable foreign body, and so many of the creatures, particularly in the summer roosts, try to remove them with their sharp teeth. They bite at the metal so vigorously that the numbers and letters engraved upon it become illegible. The band can prove harmful if the bat compresses it in such a way that it injures the wing membrane or causes swelling of the forearm. Opinions differ on the extent of losses brought about in this way. Undoubtedly, banding represents a disturbing factor in the life of a bat, and therefore, in some countries, marking is no longer carried out on those species in which numbers are declining seriously. In the remaining species, every attempt is made to ensure that banding is carried out carefully, with no unnecessary disturbance in the roost. And certainly while the females are pregnant or suckling young, no programme of banding should be initiated.

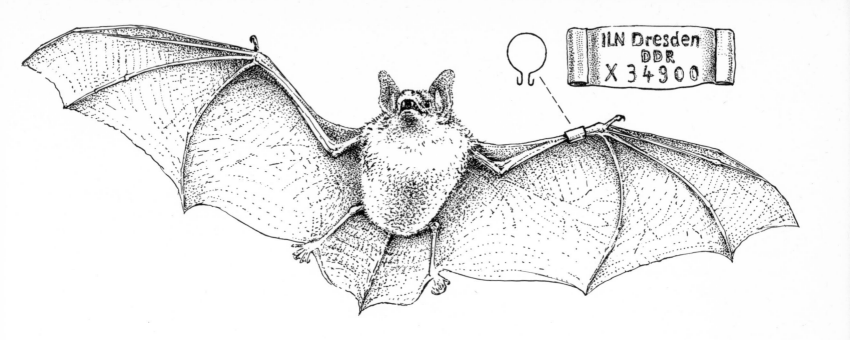

Bat band (arm clip). The band is applied to the forearm and can provide valuable scientific information.

Much of the information on individual species of bats that can be provided by banding has already been obtained for a large number of populations, and in these cases, banding should be restricted.

What information has banding provided?

Bat banding has provided valuable information, particularly when it has been possible to mark very large numbers of one species; because of the secretive habits of bats, only a small proportion of those banded are recovered.

When it is calculated that over the whole world, some millions of bats of a wide variety of species have been banded (in the U.S.A. alone, more than 162,000 Guano bats between 1952 and 1967 and in Europe well over 60,000 Mouse-eared bats), it seems an enormous total. But banding on such a scale is necessary when one considers that the number of long-distance recoveries is very small. The first recoveries of banded bats that had met with an accident or had been found in the course of checks on summer and winter roosts, provided interest-

ing information on the quarters, what direction they take in the flight to the summer roost and how far it is from the summer to the winter home.

Recoveries of Large Mouse-eared bats banded by Eisentraut showed that they end their winter rest and set off on the flight to the maternity colonies in early spring (March/April). Not infrequently, sudden cold spells at this time catch them unawares and can prove fatal.

Although there are both species that are fond of travelling and others that are sedentary, it is not possible to say that the former always cover long distances to get to their summer grounds. Whether they migrate, and how far they travel, depends very much upon the habitat and the available living quarters. In places where ideal summer and winter quarters lie close together, the move is often a local one of no more than a few kilometres. It can even happen that in summer, the cellar is simply exchanged for the attic within the same house. But this is rare. Usually the site of the maternity colony lies further from the winter roost than this.

How far the bat migrates, depends upon its flight capacity. It is much easier for species that are powerful fliers, such as the Common Noctule (*Nyctalus noctula*) to cover long distances than it is for species with a weaker flight behaviour. Included here are, for example, Long-eared bats (*Plecotus*) and Horseshoe (*Rhinolophus*). In summer, the latter travel only a few kilometres from their winter roosts. Observations carried out over a number of years in England by the Hoopers showed that the Greater Horseshoe bat (*Rhinolophus ferrumequinum*), which is one of the larger species of European bats, rarely covers more than 30 kilometres in its seasonal migrations. Its summer roosts lie in the neighbourhood of the caves which in winter are vitally important to this bat. The zoologist Roer of Bonn divides European cave-dwelling and arboreal bats according to their migratory habits into three groups: 1. species committed to their habitat, 2. species with moderately well-developed migratory instincts, and 3. species with strong migratory tendencies.

He includes Horseshoe bats in the first group. It has been found that, like its larger relations in England, the Lesser Horseshoe bat (*Rhinolophus hipposideros*), which has been observed on the northern edge of the Hercynean Mountains and the Alps, also travels no more than 30 kilometres at most from its winter roost.

Most European species show a fairly marked inclination to migrate. The principal members of this group are the Large Mouse-eared bats (*Myotis myotis*). In summer, they are able to travel up to 100 kilometres, or even more, from their underground winter quarters. The limit of their distribution can extend further northwards if suitable caves are available there as winter quarters. Mine galleries or quarries built by man are often selected as the winter roost.

Barbastelles (*Barbastella barbastellus*) behave in a similar way to Large Mouse-eared bats. They also cover distances of up to 100 kilometres. Individuals have been found up to 150 kilometres north of the winter roosts. Geoffroy's bat (*Myotis emarginatus*) spends the winter in large numbers inside systems of caves in Southern Limburg (Netherlands). Recoveries of bats banded here have shown that they spread out in summer in a northwesterly to northeasterly direction, covering distances of up to 100 kilometres.

Pond bats (*Myotis dasycneme*) which also spend the winter in these caves, belong to the group of species with strong migratory tendencies. Since they are found very frequently in northern Europe in summer, while the caves that are their winter quarters lie on the fringes of the Hercynian Mountains, it is clear that they must cover 200 kilometres or more twice every year. The Long-winged bat (*Miniopterus schreibersi*) is also known to undertake extensive migrations. Some that were banded in the winter roost near Barcelona (Spain), were recovered in the south of France. They had flown northwards a distance of about 350 kilometres.

While banding Large Mouse-eared bats in the Berlin area in the thirties, Eisentraut found that in spring they fly in a northerly direction up to 200 kilometres from their winter roosts. Of the Common Noctules (*Nyctalus noctula*) that spent the winters in the Church of Our Lady in Dresden until 1945, the most distant recovery was reported from Lithuania. This bat had covered 750 kilometres in a north-northeasterly direction. Since then, large numbers of bats have been banded in many European countries, providing much information on the migratory behaviour of various species. Observations made by the Soviet zoologist Strelkov are particularly interesting. He has reported autumn migrations of Common Noctules in which distances of more than 500 kilometres have been covered. A record performance was established by a female Noctule that was banded in August 1957 near Voronezh, and was recovered at the beginning of January 1961 in southern Bulgaria, at a distance of 2347 kilometres from the banding site. Because of the interval of several years between banding and recovery, it is not certain whether the bat covered this distance in the course of a single migration.

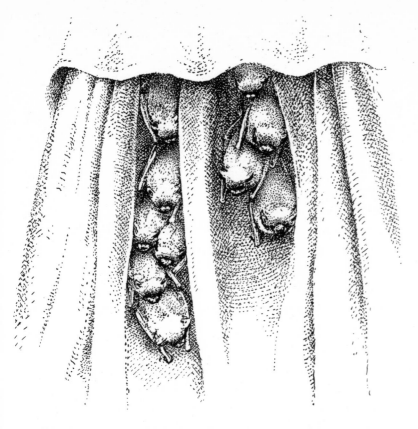

On their autumn migrations, Pipistrelles *(Pipistrellus pipistrellus)* sometimes take up temporary quarters in rooms in houses. But the discovery of a group of these small creatures one morning among the folds of the curtains is no cause for panic.

Some remarkable recoveries have also been made in Bulgaria and Greece of Pipistrelles *(Pipistrellus pipistrellus)* that had been banded in the Ukraine. They had flown in autumn more than 1000 kilometres in a south-southwesterly direction. It is possible that the extreme cold of a continental winter compels the bats to undertake such long journeys. Long-range migrations have also been reported for Pipistrelles that had been banded in the German Democratic Republic. A female, banded at the end of July 1970 near Neubrandenburg was recovered as early as November of the same year in Saint-Dizier (France). In just over three months, it had covered about 770 kilometres in a southwesterly direction.

The migratory behaviour of the small Pipistrelles remains something of an enigma, for it is known that many members of this genus living in Central Europe make no long-distance flights and can be classified as decidedly committed to their local habitat.

The correct interpretation of recoveries made at such distances as those quoted is difficult. Since they are usually single finds, they should initially be considered as exceptions. It is hardly possible that such vast distances need to be covered to find suitable winter quarters. But the possibility cannot be ruled out that in certain regions, the pressure of population becomes so great that the bats are forced, not to migrate, but to emigrate.

The large number of recoveries of banded bats shows that it is not possible to determine a fixed direction of migration. Depending upon the location of the winter roost, it can take the bats in various directions. The northern European species usually migrate south in autumn, since it is not until they reach the Central Mountains that they find ideal winter quarters.

As a result of bat banding and the regular check on the roost which it entails, it has also been found that bats are very faithful to one locality. Whether they undertake major migrations or remain throughout the year in the same district, they are still found again every summer in the same maternity colonies, and in winter, banded bats are discovered once again in the same cave in which they were banded. For this reason, banding has been able to provide information on the longevity of bats.

Long-distance orientation—an unsolved riddle

When bats have to cover very long distances to reach new quarters, they apparently make use of familiar migratory routes. This does not prevent them from interrupting their migratory flights for short periods of rest in intermediate roosts. The details of migration remain something of a mystery. Little is known about how the bats migrate, whether individually, in small groups or in mass

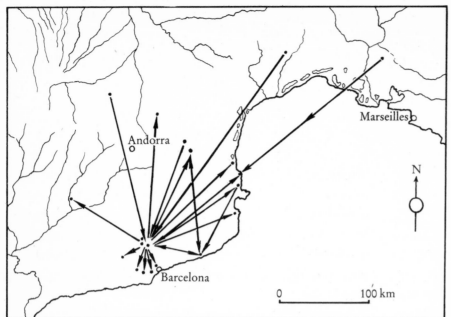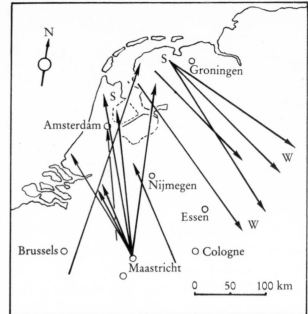

Migratory routes of European bats (after Roer, 1967),
a Migration routes of Long-winged bats *(Miniopterus schreibersi)* that were
marked at the Banding Centre of *Avenc del Davi* near Barcelona. Arrows
indicate the direction of flight within the area of northern Spain and southern France, from the place of banding to the point of recovery.
b Many Pond bats *(Myotis dasycneme)* in the Netherlands have their winter
roost (W) in the caves of Southern Limburg (near Maastricht) and migrate
northwards in spring to their summer roosts (S).

flights. It is possible that the distinctly gregarious nature
of most species causes them to remain together in fairly
large groups. But how is it possible for the young of a
population to find the accustomed winter roost? Do they
rely upon the "local knowledge" of the older bats until
they themselves have imprinted the migratory route upon their memory, or can they manage without any adult
guidance?

Eisentraut was the first to demonstrate the extent to
which bats remain true to the original roost, in a series of
large-scale "homing" experiments. If Large Mouse-
eared bats were removed from one winter roost to another, they usually remained there for that particular winter, but by the following one, they had already returned
to roost with the members of the same species in the original home. Even when they were transported for distances of up to 150 kilometres, they were found the next
winter in the original roost once more. Homing experi-

ments carried out since then in other countries have confirmed Eisentraut's findings. The highest record in such
an experiment is held by certain Big Brown bats *(Eptesicus fuscus)* in the U.S.A., which found their way home
over a distance of almost 700 kilometres. A Common
Noctule that was taken from its summer roost in Lund
(Sweden) to Gothenburg 237 kilometres away, was
found once again in Lund the following year. Another
Noctule, released 125 kilometres from Amsterdam, appeared back at its home roost only two days later. On the
other hand, homing experiments with Lesser Horseshoe
bats, carried out both in Poland and in the Federal Republic of Germany, showed that at distances of more
than 20 kilometres, the bats were unable to find their way
back to their roosts. It is important not to generalize too
widely from the results of these homing experiments,
since in all cases, only a certain percentage of the released
animals were found again in the original roosts. The
greater the distances, the fewer bats could be shown to
have returned.

Nevertheless, the results show that it is rarely possible
to rid a house of bats simply by catching them and releas-
ing them at another place. It should surprise no one if, a
few days later, the small lodgers are found once again
hanging in their accustomed roost in the attic.

This roost loyalty does not prevent bats from moving
to new quarters. They are sensitive to every detail of their

172

habitat, and either in summer or winter, may well remove quite suddenly, often for no obvious reason, to a new home.

The attachment to the chosen roost on the one hand, and on the other the fact that most species travel quite long distances between summer and winter quarters, raise the question of how bats are able to find their way when they migrate. Just as ornithologists try to solve the problem of long-distance orientation in migratory birds by means of observation and ringing, so, too, the question arises for the bat specialist of what are the sensory systems and criteria that help bats to find their way back to the place from which they set off.

Birds migrate by day and by night. They appear to orientate themselves particularly by the position of the sun, but there is increasing evidence of the importance of the earth's magnetic field. How can a bat manage, since it is active only at night? Can it make use of its system of echolocation in finding its way over great distances? It is known that bats are able to build up excellent sound-memory pictures of the immediate area of their biotope, using their system of echolocation. But it is impossible to say whether they are capable of storing memory pictures of this kind of the thousands of square kilometres they cover in the course of migration. It may be that bats possess some kind of sensory receptors for long-distance orientation that we are not yet able to recognize and analyze.

To begin with, the possibility cannot be ruled out that, even over wide areas, bats may learn to recognize salient features of the countryside, and use them as a means of orientation on their seasonal migratory flights. Yet the bats that were transported inside closed boxes in the homing experiments had no opportunity to familiarize themselves with the surroundings during the journey, and nevertheless, at least some of the bats found their way home.

It may be that they possess a sense of direction that acts like the needle of a compass, showing them which way to fly to reach the summer or winter roost. Do they perhaps take their bearings from the moon or stars, or even from variations in the brightness of the sky at dusk and at dawn? We do not know yet.

There is no doubt that migration and the system of orientation involved are instinctive. But certain learning processes obviously play a part in comprehending the environment. This would explain why older bats reach their destination with a higher success rate and in a shorter length of time.

In this sphere, a number of important questions still remain unanswered. Further observation and new methods of research are needed to explain this intriguing phenomenon in the life of bats.

Scientific methods employed today include that of attaching miniature transmitters to the backs of bats in order to record with a high degree of accuracy a continuous account of daily routine, migratory routes and speed of travel, in short, the entire activity of a population. Such techniques are already producing interesting information and promise exciting results in the future.

Bats need friends

By no means all aspects of the biology of bats have yet been explained. A number of interesting questions still remain, but will they ever be answered? With today's rapid developments in science and technology, there would appear to be cause for optimism, were it not for the sobering realization that the very existence of the bat is threatened.

Many species of the temperate latitudes, which to a large extent inhabit the highly developed industrial countries of the Old and the New World, have been showing a steady decline in numbers over the last fifteen to twenty years. The reasons for the drastic reduction in the stock of these harmless and indeed useful creatures are not only those depicted in the opening chapter of this book, namely, fear and superstition, but the increasingly rapid alterations in environmental conditions which provide the bats with scarcely any opportunity to come to terms with the new situation.

For a group of animals which has evolved so many different forms of specialization over the last 50 million years, it is not easy to adapt, overnight as it were, to new living conditions. Therefore it is urgently necessary to help the cause of bats, not only because, like every living creature, they are entitled to their place in nature, but because in many ways, directly and indirectly, they contribute to the affairs of men, both in the field of medicine and of economics.

Their value to medicine is no longer that of providing the basis of "cures" in the form of essences and salves; rather is it a question of turning certain abilities and skills that bats have evolved to the benefit of mankind as well. The discovery of ultrasonic orientation in bats opened up a field of research into the possibility of equipping blind people with a system of echolocation to facilitate spatial orientation and the perception of obstacles. Future experiments with bats will show how the creatures are able not only to locate objects, but also to differentiate the forms and structures of those objects. The solution of these problems may allow blind people one day to perceive the details of their surroundings by the use of technology akin to the system evolved by bats millions of years ago.

Research into all the metabolic processes on which hibernation is based is of paramount importance to medicine. Surgery carried out at a lowered body temperature with reduced consumption of oxygen, presupposes a knowledge of the control mechanisms and possible attendant symptoms of hypothermia. In addition, it has been found that in hibernation, animals age less rapidly and show increased resistance to infection. There is also a reduced susceptibility to X rays. These findings may also help to extend the biological potential of man. As a final example drawn from the biology of Chiroptera, one might well mention sperm conservation and delayed foetal development during hibernation. In this sphere, bats have been employing mechanisms for thousands of years which man has only just started to use in animal breeding, and which could even have valuable implications for human reproduction.

The role of bats in the economic sphere is probably of even greater importance. This is associated with their feeding habits. For example, in their area of distribution, the nectar- and pollen-eating species make a valuable contribution to the pollination of chiropterophile flowers and shrubs. But it is the insectivorous species that have particular economic value. Analysis of the food spectrum and of the amount of food consumed shows that the activities of these nocturnal hunters are of great benefit to forestry and agriculture. Depending upon their numbers, they can devour many hundredweights of insects annually, most of which are exclusively nocturnal and include many that are plant pests.

Since hardly any insectivorous birds are active at night, bird and bat complement one another as agents of biological pest control. The energy consumption of bats is high and their appetite is accordingly great. Large species, such as Large Mouse-eared bats and Common Noctules, consume more than 30 cockchafers each in the course of one night, so it is easy to see what vast quantities of insects large colonies demolish in the summer months. It is said that the American Little Brown bat *(Myotis lucifugus)* can eat 65 moths or 500 gnats in an hour. Noctules in captivity have devoured 115 mealworms in half an hour. This represents about a third of the animal's own body weight. Since digestion is rapid, the stomach is soon empty again and the search for food is renewed. A colony of 100 Noctules consumes an estimated 15 kg of insects during a single summer.

The numbers of bats in most regions of the temperate latitudes are, however, now too small to play a decisive part in pest control and thereby to contribute to maintaining a balanced ecological community. For a long time now, the use of chemicals has been widespread in agriculture and forestry as the principal means of protecting crops and stored foods from pests. It has been estimated that today, about 20 per cent of the world's crops are destroyed by insects. Although measures of chemical pest control are undoubtedly necessary, it is at the same time important to seize any opportunity of reducing their use. Chemical pest control spreads poison not only among specific pests but also throughout the whole environment, for it is impossible to avoid destroying useful creatures together with the pests. So every effort should be made to find an alternative to the use of chemicals against plant pests and, particularly in tropical areas, against insects of medical importance, and increasingly to develop and employ various biological methods of controlling harmful organisms. This includes measures to conserve and increase the numbers of natural enemies of pests.

Since bats consume such vast numbers of insects, they also produce considerable quantities of droppings, and these have proved very valuable. They accumulate under the roosts of large colonies as dunes of guano several metres high. The value of bat dung to agriculture, on account of its high nitrogen content, was recognized in America at about the turn of the century, and the commercial mining of bat guano began. In the first forty years of this century, a fertilizer company in California removed from caves during the winter months more than 100,000 tons of this organic fertilizer. Bats enabled the owners to amass a considerable fortune. In Europe and Africa (with the exception of Kenya), guano mining has not achieved commercial importance. But huge deposits of it are known to exist in Australia and Southeast Asia.

In the Carlsbad Caverns of New Mexico, U.S.A., layers of guano some 15 m in depth cover several hundred square metres of the floor of the caves beneath the roost of Guano bats *(Tadarida brasiliensis)*. Examinations carried out by palaeontologists and archaeologists show that Guano bats have spent the summer in these caves for about 17,000 years, in which time they have produced these vast mountains of droppings.

The accumulations of guano had economic value during the American Civil War. In this case, they were mined not for the purpose of obtaining fertilizer, but for the extraction of nitrate from the guano for the manufacture of gunpowder.

This example of the indirect exploitation of bats is part of history. More topical are the culinary habits of certain people in Africa and Asia, who eat bats. Members of expeditions have reported that in various parts of these continents, large species of Flying Foxes in particular are hunted, because their flesh is considered a delicacy.

Many dangers threaten bat numbers

Bats need friends because they are endangered. Bat specialists in various countries of Europe, U. S. A. and Canada report with concern that in their countries, the existence of the creatures is threatened by a variety of direct and indirect dangers. In spite of this, not all European countries have placed the Chiroptera under protection. And in the U. S. A., not all the states have enacted legislation for the protection of bats.

But legal measures alone cannot ensure the preservation of bats. Only if man himself is prepared to take positive action to safeguard the existence of bats and their roosts and to ward off dangers that threaten them, is there any chance that these curious mammals will be preserved.

However, alterations that are made to the environment of many populations of bats are often so radical that the bats are no longer able to adapt to the new conditions. Structural changes to the roosting areas and the intensive use of land for agriculture have far-reaching consequences on the life of bats. Since bats make very specific demands on climatic conditions, on the nature of the roost and on the food that is available, they react with particular sensitivity to alterations made to their habitat. In the role of biological indicators, they can provide important information on the extent to which a balance exists between the ecological and economic aspects of the increasing industrialization that also prevails in agriculture and forestry.

The decline in the numbers of bats in many European countries indicates that this balance has been disturbed. The ecological quality of our environment has deteriorated.

As early as 1972, a report from England showed that the numbers of Greater Horseshoe bats (*Rhinolophus ferrumequinum*) had declined in the last 15 years by 80 to 90 per cent. At the end of the seventies, word came that the Lesser Horseshoe bat (*Rhinolophus hipposideros*) had become extinct in the Federal Republic of Germany. In spite of legal measures of protection, information provided to the public and special care of the roosts, it had not been possible to prevent the disappearance of this species.

In 1977 the Bonn zoologist Roer assessed the population trends in bats in the Federal Republic of Germany and reached the alarming conclusion "that in addition to Horseshoe bats, many other species also show a considerable decline, and that bats as a whole are endangered". The decline in the number of individuals living in the roosts of the Large Mouse-eared bat (*Myotis myotis*) is particularly striking. In many places in the Federal Republic of Germany, there are now only 10 per cent of the bats that lived there 15 years ago. A similar decline in numbers is seen among Large Mouse-eared bats throughout Western Europe and to a lesser extent Eastern Europe.

What are the particular reasons for this reduction? People still continue to persecute bats, since they do not feel comfortable about living under the same roof as the creatures. "Weird" noises and the soiling of the roosts are the excuses they make for driving out bats or moving them to different roosts. The latter practice is usually unsuccessful, since bats always return to the roosts they have used for decades or even centuries, and remain true to them. If it is absolutely necessary, for reasons of hygiene, to remove bats from a roost, first consult an expert. Perhaps the best way is to estimate the number of bats flying out on one or two evenings and then bar all means of access to the roost on a subsequent evening after counting the bats that fly out. Since not all the bats will necessarily have emerged on the first night, the main

106   Hibernatory community of the Lesser Horseshoe bat *(Rhinolophus hipposideros)* in a cave in Czechoslovakia. In their roost, Horseshoe bats do not bunch together but space themselves with intervals between individuals. All the bats have enveloped themselves in their flight membranes.

107   Hibernatory community of Long-winged bats *(Miniopterus schreibersi)* in a cave in Czechoslovakia

108   Mediterranean Horseshoe bats *(Rhinolophus euryale)* hibernating on the roof of a cave in Czechoslovakia.

109   Greater Horseshoe bats *(Rhinolophus ferrumequinum)* hibernating in a cave in England

179

110 Hibernating Daubenton's or
Water bats *(Myotis daubentoni)*.
Note the identification bands on
the forearm of many of the bats.

111 Brown Long-eared bat *(Plecotus auritus)* in hibernation.
Frequently the bats roost individually in rock crevices. The large ears
are concealed beneath the wings;
what appears like an ear is the tragus.

112 Bechstein's bat *(Myotis bechsteini)*. This large-eared species
does not fold its ears away when it
sleeps. Bechstein's bat is found
rather rarely in Europe.

113   Greater Horseshoe bat *(Rhinolophus ferrumequinum)*. Typical hibernatory position. The wing membranes are wrapped round most of the body but the face is left free.

114   Large Mouse-eared bat *(Myotis myotis)* hibernating. Wing and tail membrane are drawn in close against the body. The small thumbs can be seen clearly.

115 Large Mouse-eared bat *(Myotis myotis)* hibernating. These bats often roost in places with very high humidity so that they become covered over with droplets of water.

116 Albinism is not unknown among bats. Here is a white Daubenton's or Water bat *(Myotis daubentoni).*

117 A Long-eared bat is banded. The wing clip is placed round the right forearm and carefully pressed together.

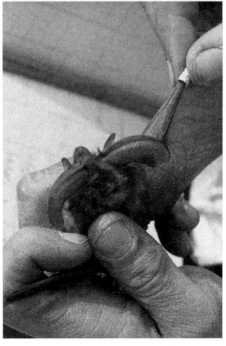

Following page:
118 Bats found in winter roosts are identified, weighed, measured and banded. Finally they are hung on the walls of the caves from which position they can return to their preferred roosts.

119 A check is made on a winter roost. Many bats crawl into deep rock crevices and can be extracted only by means of special pincers.

120 A Northern bat *(Eptesicus nilssoni)* has become entangled in a mist net. Only since extremely fine synthetic fibres have been used in the manufacture of nets has it been possible to catch bats by netting them. The threads are so fine that they cannot be located by the bat's "radar" system.

121 Bat roosting and breeding boxes. These are intended to encourage colonization by woodland bats, particularly in coniferous monocultures.

122 Inspecting a bat box

123 If a box is occupied, a gauze sack is attached beneath it to catch the bats. In this way they are collected, identified and banded.

accesses should be opened again the next evening. This should not be done between mid-June and late August when dependent young may be left in the roost. Nor should it be done during cold wet weather when few bats will emerge and those that do may have difficulty in finding alternative accommodation. Constant illumination of the roost can also cause the bats to move away. Certainly these methods are less unpleasant for the animals and householders than the ill-considered use of poison or gas. In any measures taken to remove bats from their roosts, it is worth considering whether the damage done to them does not outweigh the minor inconvenience to a few people of the bats' presence.

It is quite certain that every roost that is lost reduces the numbers of bats even further. This is equally true of tree-dwelling and of house bats. The modern forester in his efficiently managed forests tolerates no ancient and diseased trees, which often contain natural hollows and the nesting holes of woodpeckers. Yet it is in precisely these holes that certain species of bats like to set up their summer roosts; frequently they also spend the winter there.

Although no statistics are available on the population trends for bats in tropical forests, it is quite certain that recent extensive programmes of forest clearing in South America, Africa and Asia must increasingly restrict the habitats of the indigenous bat populations, and therefore reduce bat numbers in the tropical regions as well.

The loss of roosts in old buildings also leads to constant reduction in the number of maternity colonies to be found there. Nowadays, old buildings are demolished or often repaired in such a way that bats are denied access. In tropical countries, where bats in their thousands inhabit ancient sacred buildings, their existence is also threatened, because of the widespread reconstruction of these ancient architectural monuments as tourist attrac-

tions. If the bats manage to find another roost there, the smell of their urine is found to be unacceptable, and the daily work of removing droppings excessive. How much simpler it is to drive the creatures away or to destroy them!

Modern methods of building, both in towns and in rural areas, frequently do not suit the living requirements of bats. High, spacious roof frames made of timber are replaced by severe concrete structures. Window shutters and ornamental detail on houses, that are favourite hiding places for many species, are found only rarely today.

Programmes of timber preservation and insect control carried out in old buildings hardly ever take into consideration the bat populations of hundreds or thousands of individuals that may well be destroyed in the process. The danger to the bats does not exist only while such treatments are being carried out, but even months later, bats can absorb the poisons through contact with roof beams or rafters.

The loss of suitable winter roosts in the form of caves, mine galleries and other underground structures also has a detrimental effect on bat numbers. Added to this are disturbances of different kinds occurring during hibernation, either because systems of caves are visited all too frequently by speleologists, tourists, children and young people, or scientists studying bats, or as a result of the commercial use of old systems of mine workings and cellar vaults. The French zoologist Brosset reported that some 9000 bats of 11 species were living in the Rancogne cave (Western France) in 1950. Ten years later, they had almost all disappeared since the cave was visited by increasing numbers of biologists, speleologists and tourists. In many places, entrances to caves and systems of galleries are sealed off tightly, for reasons of safety, without any thought being given to bats that are imprisoned there or permanently excluded from their roosts.

185

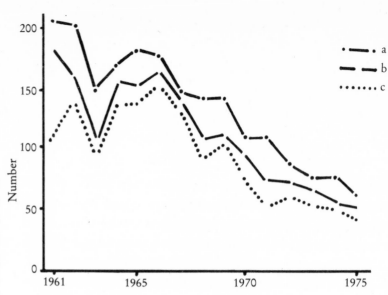

Decline in number of Large Mouse-eared bats (*Myotis myotis*) over a period of 15 years in a maternity colony consisting of three separate roosts, in the Eifel (Federal Republic of Germany) (after Roer, 1977)
a number of adult females, b total number of births, c number of surviving young

Modern agricultural practices effect both alterations to the biotope of bats and increasing deterioration in the supply of insect food. Extensive systems of monoculture, the removal of thickets from fields, measures of soil improvement, the drainage of small bodies of water and pools, and the implementation of unrestricted programmes of weed control reduce drastically the total numbers and the number of species of insects. In certain test areas in England, a decline of 50 per cent in the number of flying insects due to environmental factors was ascertained for the years 1947 to 1953.

In certain places within the countries of Central and South America, measures for the control of Vampire bats are not concentrated exclusively on this family, and here a great many harmless species of bats have also been destroyed. It is reported from Venezuela that in the sixties, 2.7 million bats of all species living there were killed in this way. In Brazil, as part of an anti-rabies campaign, all the bats living in 8240 caves were gassed or buried alive within a period of 5 years. The same has occurred in the Middle East in attempts to control fruit-eating Rousette bats.

Insecticides are not exclusively a benefit to man

Probably the greatest danger that threatens bats results from the use of pesticides. These are chemical poisons used in many countries to control animal and plant pests in agriculture and forestry. One group of these poisons comprises the insecticides, of which DDT has become known world-wide. In many countries, particularly in the tropics, it has primarily been used for some time, and still is today, to destroy pests of medical importance, such as Mosquitoes, Sand-flies, Black-flies and Tsetse flies. But unfortunately it also kills all other insects, useful and insignificant.

It soon became clear that the excessive and uncontrolled use of measures of insect control is harmful both to higher animals and to man. Since even slight quantities in the body can be fatal, there were losses among domestic animals, fish died and innumerable birds were destroyed in the U.S.A., where the product was used very intensively in the years around 1960. The decline in numbers in the large bat colonies became increasingly apparent. It was only now that the danger of the introduction of the poison into the food chains was recognized.

Many of our bats, large numbers of birds and other vertebrates live on insects that show traces of these poisons in their body. Many insects are no longer affected by the poison; they have long since established resistance to it. But in the digestive process, the insecticides enter the body of the vertebrates where they are stored in fatty organs. Since it is virtually impossible for DDT, for example, to be broken down within the body, its concentration increases over a period of time. As long as these materials remain in the fatty tissue, they are harmless.

But if the body's fat reserves are reduced rapidly, as happens regularly in bats in the course of arousal from hibernation and during spring and autumn migrations, high concentrations of poison enter the circulation and reach the brain, where they have a damaging or even fatal effect. For our indigenous bats, the danger is particularly great in spring, since at the end of hibernation, they are already weakened and are scarcely able to cope with additional physical stresses.

Examinations carried out by American workers of the Big Brown bat *(Eptesicus fuscus)* have shown that these animals are significantly more sensitive to DDT than other mammals that were tested. At the end of hibernation, the lethal dose *(dosis letalis)* was between 25 and 40 mg/kg, whereas for rats, the lethal dose was between 200 and 800 mg/kg and for mice, between 175 and 450 mg/kg. Experiments carried out on Pipistrelles showed that in summer, sensitivity to chlorinated hydrocarbons is also greater than in other mammals.

On the basis of these findings, the accumulation of insecticide residues in the bodies of bats must be considered a substantial cause of the drastic decline in numbers or even the extermination of these creatures in many countries.

In her book *Silent Spring* (1962), the American biologist Rachel Carson first drew attention to the damage that had been caused to birds by the use of insecticides. Only the specialists realized that a similar startling balance sheet could be drawn up for bats. The absence of bird song in the spring might well cause general alarm, but who notices the presence or the numbers of bats flitting through parks and gardens in the evening.

American workers have reported that the Eagle Creek Cave in Arizona houses what is probably the world's largest colony of Guano bats *(Tadarida brasiliensis)*. In summer 1964, it was estimated that there were 25 million individuals there; to satisfy numbers of this kind would require 40 tons of insects a night. In June 1970, this maternity colony comprised only 600,000 bats. This means that for every 40 animals in 1964, only one was there six years later. And it is not only among Guano bats that this situation exists.

In the early seventies, the list of endangered and increasingly rare species already included 22 of the 78 species or subspecies living in the U. S. A. In addition to insectivorous bats, the blossom-visiting species are affected equally, since in many places they come into direct contact with the insecticides.

The annihilation of bat populations, as of other animals, does not begin when they die as a result of poisoning which has reached them through the food chain, but starts with the fact that even slight amounts of poison impair reproductive capacity and can lead to sterility. Since bats in any case have a low reproduction rate, this factor is vitally important for the preservation of the species. The new-born young are particularly threatened, since with their mother's milk, they absorb poisons which build up within their bodies, at a time when they are not able to go out and find their own food.

Since that time, the use of certain insecticides, particularly DDT, has been prohibited or restricted in many countries. In order to eliminate the dangers inherent in the chemicals, it would be necessary to develop rapidly degradable materials that are quite specific in their action. Another way, which in the interests of maintaining a healthy environment it is essential for us to pursue, is the extension of the practice of biological pest control.

The protection of bats—
an urgent task of Nature Conservation

The multiplicity of dangers to which bats are exposed and the resulting decline in numbers that has been reported in the last twenty years from many different countries, raise the question of whether there still remains any possibility at all of saving these useful animals in the Palaearctic and Nearctic regions from destruction.

Even if economic and ecological demands cannot always be reconciled, our awareness of the causes of the danger that threatens should make it possible for us to alleviate that danger, even if only partially.

Protection of the winter roost by fixing a grating over the entrances and exits to systems of caves and galleries.

In addition to legal measures of protection for bats, it is important to enlighten people and bring about an understanding of these harmless and useful mammals. Just as vital are concrete measures of protection and conservation of the bats and of their habitats.

Reports of local measures of protection in many different countries give grounds for hope that the populations living there may yet be saved. For example, the caves in Southern Limburg in the Netherlands, which for a long time have been the winter roosts of many species of bats living in north western Europe, were officially designated a Bat Protection Area by the Dutch authorities in 1970. This system of galleries comprises an area of about 40 km², in which every winter, more than 1000 bats of ten different species are found. In the thirties, Dutch workers began a large-scale programme of bat banding in these caves, and since then, have marked more than 20,000 individuals.

The Carlsbad Caverns in New Mexico, U.S.A., which in summer house such vast numbers of Guano bats, were designated a United States National Park in 1930. In this case, the reason why protection of the summer roosts was not sufficient to halt the drastic decline in numbers, was that the Guano bats here, like those in other caves, were also exposed to poisoning by DDT. In the thirties, the colony in the Carlsbad Caverns was estimated at 8 million animals. In the fifties, about 4 million bats assembled in the caves each summer. But today, numbers are estimated at 200,000 individuals.

Although the use of DDT has been prohibited in the U.S.A. for some years, the Guano bats continue to be seriously endangered during the winters spent in Mexico, where this insecticide was still being used in the seventies.

It has been pointed out in the U.S.A. that constant visits from scientists and student groups, with up to 40

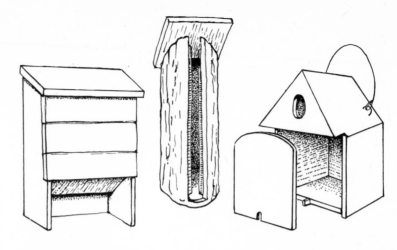

Sleeping and breeding boxes made of timber and wood concrete to encourage colonization by bats.

excursions a year, are also detrimental to large colonies of bats. Continuous disturbances of the maternity roosts upset the bats to such an extent that pregnant females frequently miscarry. If harassed, they remove to substitute roosts in which conditions are usually less favourable than those of the familiar roosts. In so doing, they may desert their young.

Protection of the winter roosts, where they occur in systems of caves or disused mine galleries, can often be achieved only by making it impossible for any unauthorized person to visit the caves. For this reason, the practice of closing off the entrance to caves has been started, while the use of firmly fixed lattice-work gates makes it possible for the bats to fly in and out freely, and for the roost attendants to visit the caves to carry out checks.

In various countries in which large numbers of roosts have been safeguarded in this way, it has been found that bat numbers have remained constant or in some cases have even increased. In carrying out such measures, it is vital that the circulation of air and the conditions of temperature inside the systems of tunnels should not be altered substantially, since bats react with great sensitivity to any change of the microclimate, and may even desert the carefully protected roost.

The necessity of providing protection for maternity colonies that are still occupied as well as for winter roosts has been taken into consideration in the nature conservation legislation of the GDR and of the U.K.

In the last 15 years, a start has been made on the provision of substitute roosts for bats. For the winter period, this is not an easy task. But the first attempts, in which hollow concrete blocks were fixed against the ceilings of unused cellars so that bats could crawl into the spaces, had a considerable success.

A simpler expedient is the construction of sleeping and breeding boxes which can provide woodland bats with an alternative roost if hollows in trees are no longer available. Bat boxes were first used in the 1930's in Eastern Europe. Species typically found in hollow trees, in the nesting holes of woodpeckers and also in the nesting boxes of birds are Common Noctules (*Nyctalus noctula*), Long-eared bats (*Plecotus* spp.), Bechstein's bat (*Myotis bechsteini*), Nathusius' Pipistrelle (*Pipistrellus nathusii*) and Pipistrelle (*Pipistrellus pipistrellus*).

In the Federal Republic of Germany in the fifties, as part of the project "Aid for the Forest", bats were encouraged to settle in artificial nesting hollows. As a substitute for old, hollow trees, suitable summer roosts were prepared in forests. Many variations on these bat boxes were developed after this in various European countries, and tried out with varying degrees of success. It is essential that they should be made of coarsely sawn timber so that the bats can climb and hang more easily on the rough surfaces of the boards. Treatment of the wood with preservatives is inadvisable, since the smell keeps the bats out of the boxes and may kill bats. In contrast to nesting boxes for birds, the most suitable entrance is in the form of a narrow slit near the floor of the box.

Experience of the use of such boxes has shown that success depends very much upon the selection of the site and the nature of the tree growth. Boxes hung in low-lying and deciduous woodlands are very rarely accepted. Here, the bats still manage to find a natural retreat. On the other hand, in forests that consist exclusively of conifers and where undergrowth is sparse, natural roosts

The bat tower built in the U.S.A. in the seventies by A. R. Rashig should help to provide additional roosting accommodation.

are few and the boxes are much used. Because bats are heat-loving animals, in summer they prefer those boxes that are warmed intensively and for long periods by the sun. Free access should not be impeded by twigs. The boxes are best hung in forest clearings protected from wind, on the edges of woods, forest lanes and paths, at a height of 4 to 6 m, facing in a south-east to south direction. Boxes facing different ways will provide roosts at different times of the year, e.g. North (East) for hibernation. Since bats are inclined to change roosts, it is advisable to put up about five boxes in one location.

Checks carried out over a number of years on bat sleeping and breeding boxes have shown that all common European species can be found using artificial roosts of this kind. Horseshoe bats are the single exception.

The provision of bat boxes has often been supported by the Forestry Authorities, since it has been recognized that the artificial colonization of bats makes a positive contribution to the control of many nocturnal insect pests. The strong attachment that bats show to a particular site is an undoubted advantage. Once they have accepted a box, it is likely that they will be found in that particular territory for a number of years.

There has been no lack of attempts to create suitable roosts for house bats. Since many species prefer spacious attics and church towers with a moderate temperature as summer roosts, a number of special bat towers have been constructed in the U.S.A. In 1911, Campbell built the first "malaria eradication guano-producing bat roost". Some very well known ones are the wooden towers built by R.C. Perky in the late twenties at Sugarloaf Key, Florida. Outwardly, they resembled huge windmills without sails. So solidly were they built that one of the towers has survived the intervening years, and can still be visited today as a tourist attraction. The towers were built to provide roosting space for half a million bats. They included a resting area, a "maternity station", a container to collect the guano and even a "cemetery".

In their day, these towers were not thought of as substitute roosts, but were to be an additional means of concentrating bats in that particular area in order to use them to control vast numbers of mosquitoes living there which transmitted malaria. At the same time, they were to provide an easy source of guano. As far as is known, bats did not settle there for any length of time. Nevertheless, it was on the model of this original tower that the zoologist R. A. Rashig constructed a similar building forty years later, but this time its purpose was to provide a roost for endangered bats. His wooden tower on the Eagle River (Wisconsin) which he built at his own expense in the early seventies, is a smaller edition of Parky's tower, designed to house only 150,000 bats. Up to 1978, Rashig had been able to observe only species of bats resting on their migratory flight, and so far it has not become a permanent summer roost. But he remains optimistic, in the knowledge that he has at least made an effort towards ensuring the preservation of bats.

Today, animal conservation is a task for which everyone should feel responsible. Yet often the measures taken are very one-sided and concentrate solely upon those animals that have a particular appeal to the wider public. But we have no right to select which animals living in the wild are to be given the chance to continue to live in today's altered environmental conditions, simply on the grounds that they are attractive or of economic importance.

Apart from the fact that bats have an undoubted economic value in eradicating insect pests, they, like every other creature, represent a link in the totality of nature with its own right to existence. If man fails to realize that he does not exist for himself alone, it is he who will one day pay the price. Man, animal, plant and landscape form a unity. They are inseparably linked and mutually dependent. It is the moral duty of all of us, for our own sake and that of our children and grandchildren, to preserve the diversity and harmony of our environment. Like the bright butterflies and the majestic birds of prey, bats, that have existed for millions of years, are equally worthy of being befriended and protected by man.

British bats and the law

In common with much of Europe, serious population declines have been observed in bats in Britain. Although this may be due partly to natural factors, these declines can also be attributed to increased disturbance of breeding roosts and hibernation sites, to their susceptibility to poisoning by pesticides and to changes in land use resulting in declines in diversity and numbers of their insect food. By the 1970s it was evident that the Greater Horseshoe bat had suffered a dramatic decline in the last 100 years, and that the Mouse-eared bat, which has never been common, was on the point of disappearing. Both species were given full protection under the Wild Creatures and Wild Plants Act 1975. However, disappearance of colonies and declines in population of monitored colonies of even our most common species, such as the Pipistrelle, were also being widely recorded. While this may partly reflect a natural fluctuation in numbers, industrialized countries often offer limited opportunities for species to recover from any population slump. Frequently the disturbance to bat sites could be avoided or minimized with a little forethought or advice. It was with such points in mind that all bat species were given very wide protection under the. Wildlife and Countryside Act 1981.

This Act has far-reaching powers. It is an offence for anyone without a licence intentionally to kill, injure or handle any wild bat in Britain, to possess a bat (dead or alive), or to disturb a bat while roosting. Licences are required for ringing, marking, photographing in the roost, selling (or offering for sale), hiring, bartering or exchanging any wild bat (dead or alive). It is permitted to tend a disabled bat in order to release it upon its recovery, or to kill humanely a seriously disabled bat which has no reasonable chance of recovery.

The law on disturbance and handling applies even in houses and other buildings. Here, as elsewhere, it is an offence to damage, destroy or obstruct access to any place that a bat uses for shelter or protection or to disturb a bat while it is occupying such a place. The only exception is that this does not apply to bats appearing in the living area of a house.

The announcement of this law and its relevance to householders led to newspaper headlines such as "An Englishman's home is no longer his castle". On the face of it this does seem a particularly restrictive law and one that will be difficult to enforce. However, all the law requires is that if work on a building is planned and might affect bats or their roost, the Nature Conservancy Council (NCC) must be informed and given the opportunity to advise and, if necessary, investigate within a reasonable period of time. It is hoped that in most cases where it is appropriate a visit can be made to assess the problem, ascertain to what degree the work is likely to disturb the bats and decide if it can be done at such a time and in such a way as to minimize disturbance to the bats. Most people prove to be sympathetic, some remain uncertain about these strange secretive creatures that they are host to, while others become very enthusiastic about "their" bats.

To help make the law effective the NCC is using the resources available in existing local interested individuals and "bat-groups" and the growing number of "bat-groups" being formed by many country Naturalists' Trusts. Not only does this give the opportunity to advise and educate, but also to get a much better idea of the numbers, distribution, population changes and roost requirements of our bat species. But most of all, "bats need friends" and this offers the opportunity to assure them as many as possible. With increased knowledge it is becoming possible to improve sites for bats and it may become more practical to encourage bats away from sites where they are unwelcome and into sites where they would be welcome.

Much remains to be learnt of these extraordinary, fascinating little animals that are a major part of our limited mammal fauna and an important part of our animal community. This law should help to ensure that they remain a significant and interesting part of our fauna.

Further information on the reasons for the law, on its rulings and advice on conservation measures can be found in a booklet available from the Nature Conservancy Council: *Focus on Bats, their Conservation and the Law*, by R. E. Stebbings and D. J. Jefferies (published by the Nature Conservancy Council, 1982). Details of the law as it affects bats can be found in section 9–11 and 16–27 of the Wildlife and Countryside Act, 1981.

Appendix

Systematic survey of bat families

Classification		Number of known living species[1]
Suborder Megachiroptera		
family Pteropodidae	Fruit bats, Flying Foxes	175
Suborder Microchiroptera		
Superfamily Emballonuroidae		
family Rhinopomatidae	Mouse-tailed bats	3
family Craseonycteridae	Hog-faced bats	1
family Emballonuridae	Sheath-tailed bats	50
family Noctilionidae	Fisherman bats	2
Superfamily Rhinolophoidea		
family Nycteridae	Slit-faced bats	11
family Megadermatidae	False Vampires	5
family Rhinolophidae	Horseshoe bats	70
family Hipposideridae	Old World Leaf-nosed bats	60
Superfamily Phyllostomoidea		
family Phyllostomidae	Spear-nosed bats	148
family Desmodontidae	Vampire bats	3
Superfamily Vespertilionoidea		
family Vespertilionidae	Vespertilionid bats	320
family Natalidae	Funnel-eared bats	8
family Furipteridae	Smoky bats	2
family Thyropteridae	American Disc-winged bats	2
family Myzopodidae	Madagascan Sucker-footed bats	1
family Mystacinidae	Short-tailed bats	1
family Molossidae	Free-tailed bats	90

[1] Data on the number of known living species differ among individual authors, particularly in families with many species (after: Pye, 1969, Koopman and Jones, 1970, Yalden and Morris, 1975, Corbet and Hill, 1980).

Distribution and principal foods of bats

Family	Area of distribution	Food
Pteropodidae	only Old World; tropics and sub-tropics from Africa to Australia	fruit, flowers, pollen
subfamily Macroglossinae	Africa, Eastern Asia	fruit juices, nectar
Rhinopomatidae	North Africa, Asia to Sumatra	insects
Emballonuridae	world-wide (pan-tropical)	insects
Noctilionidae	Central and South America (tropics)	insects, fish
Nycteridae	Africa, Eastern Asia	insects
Megadermatidae	Africa, Asia, Australia (tropics)	insects, small vertebrates
Rhinolophidae	Old World	insects
Hipposideridae	Africa, Asia, Australia (tropics)	insects
Phyllostomidae	Central and South America	insects, small vertebrates, fruit, fruit juice, nectar
Desmodontidae	Central and South America (tropics)	blood of vertebrates
Vespertilionidae	world-wide (Nearctic, Palaearctic, Africa, Australia, South America; Hawaii, Iceland, New Zealand	insects, individual species: fish and small vertebrates
Natalidae	Central America, Caribbean	insects
Furipteridae	Central America, tropical South America	insects
Thyropteridae	Central America, tropical South America	insects
Myzopodidae	Madagascar	insects
Mystacinidae	New Zealand	insects
Molossidae	world-wide (especially pan-tropical, also Southern Europe and the south of North America)	insects

Index

Bibliography

Allen, G. M.: *Bats*. Cambridge, 1939.
Baker, J. K.: *What about bats?* Carlsbad, New Mexico, 1961.
Barbour, R. W., and W. H. Davis: *Bats of America*. Kentucky, 1969.
Brentjes, B.: "Fledertiere in den Kulturen Altamerikas und des Alten Orients." In: *Milu* (1971), pp. 175–183.
Brosset, A.: *La Biologie des Chiroptères*. Paris, 1966.
Constantine, C. G.: "Bats in relation to health, welfare and economy of man." In: Wimsatt (Editor): *Biology of Bats*, 1970.
Corbet, G. B., and J. E. Hill: *A world list of mammalian species*. British Museum (Nat. Hist.), London, 1980.
Davis, W.-H.: "Hibernation: Ecology and physiology ecology." In: Wimsatt (Editor): *Biology of Bats*, 1970.
Eisentraut, M.: *Aus dem Leben der Fledermäuse und Flughunde*. Jena, 1957.
Eisentraut, M. (Editor): "Berichte und Ergebnisse von Markierungsversuchen an Fledermäusen in Deutschland und Österreich." In: *Bonner Zoolog. Beiträge*, Bonn, 1960.
Felten, H.: "Gespensterfledermaus und Röhrennasenflughund." In: *Natur und Volk*, 88 (1958), p. 361.
Geluso, K. N., J. S. Altenbach, and D. E. Wilson: "Bat mortality: Pesticide, Poisoning and Migratory Stress." In: *Science*, 194 (1976), pp. 184–186.
Grassé, P.-P.: *Traité de Zoologie*. Vol. XVII, *Mammifères*. Paris, 1955.
Greenhall, A. M., and J. L. Paradiso: *Bats and Bat Banding*. Washington, 1968.
Greenhall, A. M.: "La rage chez les chauves-souris." In: *La Revue de Médecine* (1975), pp. 751–754.
Griffin, D. R.: *Vom Echo zum Radar*. Munich, 1959.
Griffin, D. R.: *Echoes of bats and men*. 1960.
Husson, A. M.: *The bats of Surinam*. Thesis. Liège, 1962.

Koopman, K. F., and J. K. Jones: "Classification of bats." In: Slaughter and Walton (Editors): *About Bats*. Dallas, 1970, pp. 22–28.
Kulzer, E.: "Über die Orientierung der Fledermäuse." In: *Aus der Heimat*, 65 (1957), pp. 132–139.
Kulzer, E.: "Der Thermostat der Fledermäuse." In: *Natur und Museum*, 95 (1965), pp. 331–345.
Kulzer, E.: "Der Winterschlaf der Fledermäuse." In: *Umschau* (1969), pp. 195–201.
Kulzer, E.: "Der Flug des afrikanischen Flughundes *Eidolon helvum*." In: *Natur und Museum*, 98 (1968), pp. 181–194.
Kulzer, E., and A. Weigold: "Das Verhalten der Grossen Hufeisennase (*Rhinolophus ferrum-equinum*) bei einer Flugdressur." In: *Z. Tierpsychol.*, 47 (1978), pp. 268–280.
Leen, N.: *The Bat*. New York, 1976.
Lera, T. M., and S. Fortune: "Bat management in the United States." *NSS Bulletin*, 41 (1979), pp. 3–9.
Meise, W.: *Der Abendsegler*. Neue Brehm-Bücherei, No. 42, Leipzig, 1951.
Milne, L. J., and M. Milne: *Die Sinneswelt der Tiere und des Menschen*. Hamburg, Berlin, 1963.
Möhres, P.: "Bildhören – eine neuentdeckte Sinnesleistung der Tiere." In: *Umschau*, 60 (1960), pp. 673–678.
Natuschke, G.: *Heimische Fledermäuse*. Neue Brehm-Bücherei, No. 269, Wittenberg, 1960.
Norberg, U.: "Aerodynamics of hovering flight in the long-eared bat *Plecotus auritus*." In: *J. exp. Biol.*, 65 (1976), pp. 459–470.
Novick, A., and N. Leen: *The world of bats*. New York, 1970.
Pye, J. D.: "Echolocation by bats." In: *Endeavour*, 20 (1961), pp. 101–111.
Pye, J. D.: "The diversity of bats." In: *Science Journal* (1969), pp. 47–52.

Sources
of illustrations

Raths, P.: *Tiere im Winterschlaf*. Leipzig, Jena, Berlin, 1977.

Roer, H.: "Wanderungen der Fledermäuse." In: Hediger (Editor): *Die Strassen der Tiere*. 1967, pp. 102–118.

Roer, H. (Editor): "Berichte und Ergebnisse von Markierungsversuchen an Fledermäusen in Europa." In: *Decheniana*, No. 18, Bonn, 1971.

Roer, H.: "Zur Populationsentwicklung der Fledermäuse (Mammalia, Chiroptera) in der Bundesrepublik Deutschland unter besonderer Berücksichtigung der Situation im Rheinland." In: *Z. f. Säugetierkunde*, 42 (1977), pp. 265–278.

Schmidt, U.: *Vampirfledermäuse*. Neue Brehm-Bücherei, 515, Wittenberg, 1978.

Stratmann, B.: "Faunistisch-ökologische Beobachtungen an einer Population von *Nyctalus noctula*." In: *Nyctalus* (N.F.), 1 (1978), pp. 2–22.

Strelkov, P. S.: "Migratory and stationary bats of the European part of the Soviet Union." In: *Acta zool. Cracoviensia*, 14 (1969), pp. 393–439.

Turner, D. C.: *The Vampire Bat*. Baltimore, London, 1975.

Vogel, St.: "Fledermausblumen in Südamerika." In: *Österr. Botan. Zschr.*, 104 (1958), pp. 492–530.

Webster, F. A., and D. R. Griffin: "The role of the flight membrane in insect capture by bats." In: *Animal Behav.*, 10 (1962), pp. 332–340.

Webster, F. A.: *Some acoustical differences between bats and man*. Conference on sensory devices for the blind. 1967.

Wilson, D. E.: "Reproduction in neotropical bats." In: *Period. biol.*, 75 (1973), pp. 215–217.

Wimsatt, W. A.: *Biology of Bats*. 3 vols., Academic Press, London, New York, 1970.

Yalden, B. W., and P. A. Morris: *The Lives of Bats*. David and Charles, Newton Abbot, London, Vancouver, 1975.

Andera, M., Prague 114

Bilke, P., Naumburg 48, 71

Birnbaum, O., Halle (Saale) 8

Carlsbad Caverns Authorities, New Mexico 60, 61

Cerveny, J., Prague 65, 67, 112, 115, 116, 120

Devez, A. R., Gabon 18, 24

Franzen, L., Frankfort on the Main 9

Gaisler, J., Brno 66, 106, 108

Grimmberger, E., Eberswalde 14, 45, 47, 50, 51, 52, 53, 54, 72, 74, 77, 96, 97, 98, 99, 105, 113

Hooper, J., Staines 10, 101, 109

Hosking, E., London 58

Howell, D. J., West Lafayette 6, 7, 80, 81, 82

Hrabě, J., Brno 107

Klawitter, J., Berlin (West) 88

Kulzer, E., Tübingen 17, 23, 26, 33, 34, 41, 57, 75, 79, 92, 93, 94, 95, 103, 104

Kunz, T. H., Boston 70

Loskarn, P., Bülstringen 11

Mönch/OKAPIA, Frankfort on the Main 90

Morris, P., Ascot 20, 22, 29, 32, 38, 44

Museum der bildenden Künste, Graphische Sammlungen, Leipzig 3

Norberg, U., Göteborg 12, 15, 89

Ortlieb, R., Helbra 91

Publisher's archives 2, 4, 5

Pye, J. D., London 27, 35, 46, 56

Roedl, F., Valtiče 42

Roer, H., Bonn 64, 100, 102

Root/OKAPIA, Frankfort on the Main 63

Rudloff, K., Erfurt 68, 110, 111, 118, 119, 121, 122, 123

Schmidecker/OKAPIA, Frankfort on the Main 16

Schober, W., Leipzig 13, 25, 40, 49

Staatliche Kunstsammlungen Dresden, Gemäldegalerie "Alte Meister" 1

Stephan, H., Frankfort on the Main 19, 21, 28, 30, 31, 36, 37, 39, 62, 69

Tuttle, M. D., Milwaukee 43, 73

Vogel, J., Vienna 84, 85, 86, 87

Webster, F., Vermont 78, 83

Woloszyn, E. W., Cracow 55, 117

ZEFA GmbH, Düsseldorf 59, 76

Special thanks are due to all colleagues and friends who provided me with interesting and rare photographs.